THE CHRISTIAN ADVENTURE

THE CHRISTIAN
ADVENTURE

A. HERBERT GRAY, M.A., D.D.
AUTHOR OF "AS TOMMY SEES US," ETC.

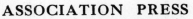

ASSOCIATION PRESS
New York: 347 Madison Avenue
1920

PRINTED IN THE UNITED STATES OF AMERICA

PREFACE

THERE are no arguments about the truth of Christianity in this book. It is wholly concerned with the preliminary question, "What is Christianity?"

I have had uncounted discussions with men and women about the truth of Christianity, and in the vast proportion of them I have found that they were talking about one thing while I was talking about another.

Sometimes I have found myself hoping devoutly that the thing which my interrogators called Christianity could *not* be proved true.

Therefore in these pages I have confined myself to an effort to present the message of Jesus as He gave it to the world. Within the limits set to me it has not been possible to do more than write a series of outlines, and I am painfully aware that no single topic has been adequately handled.

Yet I hope that what I have written may at least suggest to some that Christianity embodies the one summons to men and women that is adequate to their humanity, and that it offers to the race the one hope of solving all the problems of civilization.

Once men and women have really accepted Christianity so conceived, it is my faith that they will very soon offer to the world a demonstration of its truth beyond all challenge.

A. H. G.

CONTENTS

CHAPTER I

JESUS

THE man who would understand Christianity must begin by understanding Jesus. Churches, creeds, and theologies are secondary affairs, however important. No man can know whether or no Christianity offers him the great things which in his heart he wants until he has faced Jesus and come to know both what Jesus was, and what Jesus offers. Churches frequently make mistakes. Creeds are never more than partially successful attempts to state truths. But Jesus either was or was not the embodiment of the essential secret of life, and while churches may come and go, and while creeds may change again and again, Christianity stands or falls by mankind's judgment on Him.

His Selflessness.—Almost at a first glance Jesus presents us with a strange combination. On the one hand, He quietly assumed an absolute authority; and on the other, He was entirely without self-regard in the ordinary sense. He never sought anything for Himself, and was serene in spirit though He had no status in society, no certain means of livelihood, and no security for life itself. In most men, even though they be good men, there is an undercurrent of thought about self which every now and then becomes apparent. In Jesus no such thoughts appear. He gave Himself lavishly to others, and never seemed to stop to consider what the world might think of Him. He was so free from vanity that the opinion of men actually did not matter to Him. Such a thing as jealousy is unthinkable in connection with Him. He did not plan out a career for Himself, and of what we call personal ambition there was no trace in all His life.

He did indeed reveal to His disciples[1] that once at the beginning of His public life He had a great struggle over this matter. At that point, when a full sense of His powers first came to Him, His human self made a very stubborn effort at self-assertion. He was racked and tossed for days on end by the familiar ambitions of great human spirits. The prospects of worldly dominion and of dazzling outward fame danced before His imagination; and a fight, grim and lonely, had to be faced before He subdued self altogether. The fight may have been renewed in secret again and again in after days, but it never came to the surface. To onlookers self seemed to be dead in Him altogether. He was content even to be despised, because He sought nothing for Himself.

The ablest and most virile of men will best be able to realize how much that means. Ambition is the last infirmity of noble minds, because for them the great ambitions are possibilities. But the

---

[1] It is obvious that the disciples can only have known about the Temptation because Jesus, for reasons of His own, for once broke through His reserve and told them that tremendous story of His own inner life.

noblest mind in history attained to a complete victory over ambition. That meant a greater thing than laying down one's life in bodily death, and in that sense Jesus laid down His life at the very beginning.

On the other hand, Jesus quietly made such an assumption of authority as the world had never heard of before. He declared that by their attitude to Himself men judged themselves. He claimed to speak for God, and that in Him God was perfectly revealed. He taught no doctrine about His own nature and person, but He consistently assumed that His coming was the central event of the world's history. To confess Him before the Father was to be sure of welcome—to deny Him was to court rejection. He crowned His claim by saying that those who had seen Him had seen God. And yet even in this most arresting and mysterious part of His life a real effort after self-obliteration is discernible. "I do nothing of myself." "The Father that dwelleth in me he doeth the works." He was invariably anxious that men should look past Him to His Father.

Both these features of Jesus arrest the heart and inspire trust. He seemed to His disciples to need no credentials except Himself. It was a later age that asked for proofs, and discussed the significance of miracles, and the circumstances of His birth, and the manner of His resurrection. His first disciples trusted Him because "never man spake like this man." They were quite sure about Him simply because of what He was to their immediate vision.

His Originality.—It will astonish those who
have never really looked at Jesus but who only
know the habitual atmosphere of churches to find
that He was quite unlike the ordinary very religious
man.   He was not a preacher.   He did indeed talk
constantly about religion, because it was to Him
the happiest and the most beautiful of all possible
subjects of talk.   But He talked spontaneously as
occasion offered, and there are no continuous discourses of Jesus.[1]   He seems not to have known
any theological words.   He avoided all those special
terms which give hardness and edge to religious
truth, and preferred to trust to impressions which
were conveyed in stories and images.   He was quite
uninterested in ceremonial, and initiated no ritual
or forms of worship except the very simple words
used at the last supper.   Above all He was *not*
oppressively solemn.   He kept no special tone of
voice for speaking about God.   He was not annoyed
by the surface interests of life, which necessarily
engross people so much.   He never seems to have
wished to quench laughter, or to have felt that the
children of eternity should never be merry in time.
He did not sit through festivities refraining for
charity's sake from criticism.   He was Himself
happy in the joys of others, and it was characteristic
of Him that once when a marriage feast was in
danger of failure through the lack of wine, He took
steps to remedy the lack.   His presence heightened

[1] The Sermon on the Mount is a collection of sayings compiled
by the Evangelist.   The Johannine discourses are not in form
characteristic of Jesus at all.

joys, and those who had thought of religion as at best a dull affair had to change their ideas in the company of Jesus. His own spirit played in such homely touch with real and familiar life, that He only just escapes definite and positive humour. He must have spoken much with a smile, and often must have made others smile—the sort of smile for which a man is the better at once.

His Appreciativeness.—When we look closer into His ways we begin to see that one main secret of this strange fascination which He exercised over unspiritual and unchurchy people lay in the fact that it was His instinct and His habit to see first in any man or woman what could be appreciated—not what was open to criticism. Have you not felt about many quite good people that they have a terrible aptness in detecting what is indefensible in your life or character? Their kind but searching glances are very disconcerting. Though they are so good, it is hard to love them, and we escape from their company with relief. But the glances of Jesus were not disconcerting. He saw more good in men than they had suspected themselves. He saw in Zaccheus the possibility of a great and generous life; and once He had seen it Zaccheus saw it too, so that forthwith it sprang into being. He saw in Mary Magdalene a great woman, not yet spoiled beyond hope. And because He saw that great womanhood in her, she forthwith began to be a great woman.

Tradition has it that once when He was leaving a village with His disciples He found a crowd at the gate gathered round the carcass of a dead mongrel dog. The others present were vying with one another in pointing out its repulsive features—its loathsome skin, its bleared eyes, its misshapen legs. But when Jesus had looked He said only this, "Pearls cannot equal the whiteness of his teeth." There is a world of meaning in that story. What He saw was the one beautiful feature in the case. And He saw it *first*. He always saw it first, even in rakes, profligates, and misers. Criticism of human beings is, of course, the easiest thing in the world. A man need hardly be intelligent in order to detect what is wrong with any given character. That popular hobby called pulling other people to pieces barely requires the use of the mind at all. To note one man's uncouth accent, and another's funny walk—to detect that this man is conceited, and that man dubiously honest—to discover that that girl is plain and that other one selfish—to label a whole year of freshers or seniors or a whole college staff with their appropriate faults—these things constitute a very rudimentary form of mental exercise.

But to see in any man or woman what can be loved and valued is a very different business. And it was in that matter that Jesus was sublimely proficient. He had the seeing eye which could detect that which is of God in any human personality. Therefore, of course, He was of immense help to all whom He met. I doubt whether any one of us was ever helped or profited by anybody who began by disapproving of us. But the people who appreciate

us can do almost anything with us. And there lay
Christ's power. Rough men and light women who
were hardened to resist the scorn of the respectable
felt constrained to say, "Why, this man values and
likes us!" And forthwith they began to respect
themselves and to have a new hope in life. To have
been appreciated by Jesus might well make any man
hold up his head.

Nor was this attitude on Christ's part in any way
an affectation. I remember the time when I sup-
posed that Jesus loved all men simply because He
believed it to be His duty, and whether or no He
found in them anything to be loved. The idea was,
of course, grotesquely foolish. God Himself could
not love what is essentially unlovable. No! Jesus
loved men and women because He could always find
in them something worthy to be loved—some possibility at the worst which was a fit object even for
Divine love. He could detect in each instance that
which justified the declaration that man was made
in the image of God.

It is a fascinating exercise to try to use His
method. I remember reviewing for this purpose a
number of people of my acquaintance. I found
that one man, whom I knew to be a drunkard, was
also a very large-hearted and generous soul. Another, of whom I knew that his business activities
would scarcely stand scrutiny, was none the less a
truly and loyally affectionate husband and father.
A third, who has a notoriously vile temper, is also
honest and reliable beyond most. Another still,
who is one of the slaves of lust, is also brave and

energetic and able. Another, who appeared mean and sly and cowardly, has none the less a soul that responds to beautiful music and can live at times in a very beautiful world. One woman, who flaunts a frivolous nature in the face of the world, can serve and slave like a heroine when trouble is in the air. Another, of whom it cannot be denied that she is vain, is also a most capable and valuable citizen. A third, who is exacting and fractious at times, is none the less capable of great acts of unselfishness. Several, who are most unattractively pious, are none the less really conscientious and consistent. Certain aggressive teetotallers turned out to be behind that forbidding exterior persons of real public spirit. Certain gaunt and stern spirits of the old school were yet honest with themselves and resolute in duty as few younger spirits are. Oh yes! and in the army I have found drinkers and swearers and men of wild hooligan nature who could on occasion display such qualities of courage, gentleness, and self-forgetfulness, as might well make most church members very humble. In connection with all these people to pay attention to what was obvious was to be repelled. But also with them all further search revealed things which not only can be loved, but which ought to be loved. And this was the instinctive manner of Jesus.

Possibly there was even more meaning than I have suggested in His willingness to be the companion of outcasts—publicans and sinners, and so forth. In Jack London's great book, "John Barley-corn," he confesses that he had always found himself irresistibly drawn to the company of the sort of men who were to be found in saloons—those whom he calls the "big chesty men," and that because there was such volume and wealth of energy in them. He found them tremendously alive and direct. Whether they were good or bad, there was a strong hearty simplicity in them. If they were but raw material they were certainly genuine material. I believe Jesus felt the same fascination in the same sort of man. The rough, untutored, hearty men of Galilee appealed to His heart far more than the refined but conventional folk of Jerusalem, or the priests and Pharisees fashioned in the schools. He could get at the former because they were at least sincere. This at least is certain, that the men who felt awkward and out of place in churches, who were accustomed to speak with loud voices and in very plain language, who had learnt no conventions and acquired no polish, none the less found themselves quite at home with Jesus. Were there such an one as He now in the world, he could go into any army dining hall, into any stokehole, any shipyard, any common room, any lodging house, and his presence would not make men uncomfortable. His coming would not be resented. And his second visit would be eagerly looked for.

His Friendships.—We shall see further into His nature by thinking of His friendships. It would seem that He was always ready to begin a friendship. Zaccheus, who belonged to the same moral class as sweating employers, was no doubt a much detested man, deliberately shunned by both the

respectable and the poor. Probably no man had
made a friend of him for years. But Jesus no
sooner knew him than He insisted on becoming his
friend; and though many houses were open to Him,
it was to the house of the *bête noir* of Jericho that
He insisted on going. Of Mary Magdalene no
respectable man and no virtuous woman would ever
have thought of making a friend. She was left to
the company of those who did her no good. But
for Jesus the fact that she needed a friend was final.
I doubt if He even realized what the world might
think. One thing only He saw, and that a lonely
soul who needed the warm garment of friendship.
And at once He wrapped her in it. She should
know forthwith that one man had real friendship
to give her. No wonder she turned for ever from
those who could only traffic with lust. Bartimæus
was to the ordinary traveller just a bit of flotsam by
the shore of life's river—just something living
within a bundle of dirty rags, to be sufficiently dealt
with by a coin carelessly thrown, or a piece of food
that could be spared. It seemed to the bystanders
an affront that he should even wish to speak with
Jesus. But Jesus saw in him only another possible
friend, and what He did was just to make a friend
of him, and so doing to make another man of him.

And so it was always. He found His friends in
no one class. He did not seek out congenial spirits.
He never considered what He could get from a
friendship. It was enough for Him always that a
man or a woman needed a friend. It was His instinct and His passion to give, and to give lavishly,

of love and fellowship even to unattractive and twisted natures. He was that kind of man.

But that was not all. Having given of His friendship, He was never willing to let a friendship end. He had the bitter experience of finding that His friends failed Him. Peter, the most demonstrative of them, passionately repudiated Him at a time of crisis. Thomas, the most dogged of them, bluntly doubted at a time when Jesus was longing to find belief. The whole band of His nearest and dearest ran away in panic at the worst hour of His life. Of such unstable friends many a man would say, "If that is all they care, I have no use for them." But Jesus having begun a friendship always refused to see it end. He sent a special and kindly message to Peter, calling him back. He gathered the eleven round Him, and though they must have been shamefaced at first, He insisted on restoring the old relations. He offered Thomas all the proof his cautious nature asked. He bridged the chasm they had made by the sheer fidelity of His own affection. He was proof even against cowardice and disloyalty. So He shows in His friendships—always ready to begin—never willing to leave off.

As we know them, men are mostly touchy, exacting, and sometimes difficult even in friendship. Sometimes they are too absorbed in their own affairs to be of use to us. Sometimes they ask more than we can give. But with Jesus it was never so. He was always able to meet a friend's claims, and having loved He loved unto the end.

And yet I do not think He was of those who do not need human love. Some strong men of good will seem always willing to give and to help, but never seem to be themselves in need. They never give their friends the chance to be of use. They never come in their turn for sympathy or seal a friendship by generous taking. I do not think Jesus was of that kind. When Peter in the folly of his impetuous love sought to restrain Jesus from the way of the cross, the very passion with which Jesus repulsed him seems to me proof that He too felt the power of human love, and knew the danger of allowing love to drag us down into that softer, warmer atmosphere where heroic things cannot be done. He was almost rude to Peter just because Peter's love had power with Him. No! He was not so independent of men that their desertions could not hurt Him. They rather made the hardest trial of His hardest hour. But His love was too big, too strong to be killed even by such blows. He was that kind of man.

His Daring.—It is quite impossible to do justice in words to the courage of Jesus, but we can let the plain facts speak for themselves. Of all the other actors in the drama of His life it is reported at some point or other that they were afraid. And in each case their fears made them play a mean part. The rich, for instance, were afraid of poverty, and therefore could not deal honestly with the truths Jesus proclaimed. The priests feared for their own position, and therefore schemed to overthrow one whose teaching lessened their authority. The Pharisees

feared the people, and therefore sought out under-
hand ways of accomplishing their ends. The mob
feared their rulers, and therefore would not stand
by the man whom at times they had acclaimed with
shouts. Pilate feared Cæsar, and when he was met
by vulgar threats that unfavourable reports might
reach Rome, he succumbed and deliberately acted
against his own convictions as a judge. And lastly,
and most tragic of all, the disciples themselves hopelessly gave way to panic at the critical hour, and
stampeded away from the Lord whom they really
loved. In all these cases we see men blatantly un-
true to their own consciences, and openly resisting
their own moral convictions. And the reason in
every case was just fear—that most sinister of all
the enemies of true manhood.

Alone among them all Jesus was never afraid.
From the very beginning of His public career He
had to make decisions daily which practically made
it certain that His life would be taken. He went
abroad into the nation to declare certain great life-
redeeming truths, but they were so obnoxious to
those in authority, that very soon it became plain
that they would not tolerate this new teacher. To
go on, therefore, was really to pile the faggots for
His own martyrdom. Yet daily He did it, and we
never catch even a glimpse of the spectre of fear
stealing in and out of His life. I cannot think that
He was one of those rare men, of whom I have at
least heard, who are said never to have known what
the feeling of fear is. He was too human for that
—too fully one of us. But He was of that chosen

company who are able never to let fear come to the surface—who in spite of it go on and do their business in a cheerful spirit—who attain to complete spiritual mastery over it—who, therefore, never seem to be afraid.   There were many members of that band at the front, men who may have had their bad hours in secret, but who never showed it—men who encouraged others by making the causes of fear seem contemptible.   And they will best appreciate Jesus.   He had to do daily exactly what men at the front did, He had to go on with a round of duty which must mean death, and therefore daily He had to lay down his life.   And yet if you look closely at Him you will not see a grim and determined man, living as it were in the throes of a tragic wrestle with fate.   Oh no!   His victory over fear was far more complete than that.   You will see a serene and happy spirit, who did not pay His enemies the compliment of being even perturbed by them and their plots.

It may seem at a first glance that there could be almost nothing in common between Jesus—the Galilean peasant, the idealist martyr—and the modern British athlete, whose friends say of him with pride that he is "a good sport."   But what is this all-important quality to which we apply the epithet "sporting"?   It has not really any necessary connection with games.   It has to be applied to men who couldn't run a hundred yards in twenty seconds, or hit a cricket ball to save their lives.   It is the word we apply to men who meet life with a laugh and not a whine—who rather enjoy risks—

CHAPTER II

WHAT WAS JESUS DOING?

So far we have considered in a measure what Jesus was, but we cannot know Him till we also ask: "What was He doing? What was the central purpose of His life?" Mark's answer to that question is contained in the words, "Jesus came preaching the gospel of the Kingdom of God." His characteristic announcement was "The Kingdom of Heaven is at hand."

Plainly, then, we cannot understand either Him or His work until we know what He meant by the Kingdom of God. It is one of the most astonishing things in all Christian history that until recently so little attention was paid to the meaning of that expression, and such an infinite amount to certain metaphysical and theological mysteries about which Jesus Himself said nothing. It would be possible to be quite well informed about the theologies of many past centuries, and yet not to know what the Kingdom of God means. On the other hand, it may turn out that if we can grasp what He meant by it we may understand Jesus and the religion He has given us without disturbing ourselves over theological mysteries at all.

It may be doubted whether two per cent. of the people who attend churches have any clear conception of the meaning of this phrase which was so constantly on the lips of Jesus. It might have been expected that it would have been the very first thing to be explained to children in connection with Christianity, and that church members would receive abundant instruction about it. It would have been natural if it had filled a central place in catechisms, and in confessions of faith. But as a matter of fact, it hardly has any place at all in creeds, or catechisms. A man might read a great deal of ordinary Christian literature and never come across the expression.

Now thousands of people are asking today why it is that Christianity seems in large measure to have failed. If it is all that Christians claim it to be— if it contains the secret of the world's peace and well-being, and if it has the power of God behind it—surely it should have saved us from this present debacle. Nineteen centuries make up a long time, and after all that time of opportunity Christianity still often seems a very weak and ineffectual thing. Christians often seem a weak and negligible quantity. They could not prevent the war. They have not been able to persuade the world to a Christian settlement after the war. If they hold the secret of the world's peace and well-being they have been singularly unsuccessful in applying it.

But what if our common Christianity is in some essential respects different from Christ's Christianity! What if in His name we have been proclaiming something less and even something different from the Gospel of the Kingdom of God! That would at least explain the disconcerting facts of today. It may be that He had the secret and that we have not had it. It may be that from very early times we have taken from Him so much less than He meant to give that the religion we have professed and practised is actually a religion without power.

It may be; and at all events the possibility ought to send us back to the gospels with a new determination to find out what actually was the authentic Gospel of the Kingdom of God, which occupied all the attention of Christ Himself. What, then, did Jesus mean by the Kingdom of God? I think a partial answer at least is to say that He used that phrase as a description of what human life becomes when it is lived under the constraint of two truths— the Fatherhood of God, and the Brotherhood of man. Those were the two great truths He came to reveal both by life and by death, and when any man fully receives them and lives under their dominion he enters the Kingdom. When any group of people live in that way then the Kingdom appears as a social fact in this life.

Another way in which Jesus put the same truth was to say that there are only two great commandments—to love God and to love one's neighbour. And when any man begins to obey those commandments he enters the Kingdom. The Kingdom means human life dominated through and through by love. To a certain extent the Kingdom comes into being when even one man achieves that kind of life. It began to come when Jesus Himself came, and individuals can realize many of its blessings in their own lives even though they are isolated individuals. And yet the Kingdom cannot fully come for any individual until others also have entered it. It is essentially a social thing. It means a society of a certain kind. Indeed, it cannot fully come until all men have entered it, and life the wide world over is life dominated by its principles.

And Jesus came to set up that kind of society. He came to substitute His Kingdom for all the kingdoms of the world. He came to a world very weary and very sad. Mazzini says of it: "Throughout the world was a dull sound of dissolution. All trembled; the heavens and the earth. . . . The soul of man had fled; the senses reigned alone. . . . Philosophy had sunk first into scepticism, then into epicureanism, then into subtlety and words. Poetry was transformed into satire."

All the social evils with which we are familiar were rampant in it, and others even more tragic. It was a cruel and a hard world, in which plainly life had gone wrong. Civilization itself seemed in acute danger, and many good people were so filled with despair that not infrequently they left the world by their own act. But Jesus did not despair. He said in effect, "Let us set up another Kingdom on quite other principles: let us begin to conform life to the mind of God. Let us turn the existing world upside down." His words were not the wild and windy words of a mere fanatic or dreamer.

He spoke with a calm assurance. He not only called on men to build that Kingdom: He declared it was at hand. He was not dismayed by the might of Imperial Rome, nor by all the battalions of the hosts of Mammon. Though outwardly a mere peasant without worldly experience, He lived habitually amidst these tremendous conceptions and looked out across the whole world with the eye of a conqueror. He dared to entertain the most imperial designs which any human mind has ever harboured. And all that because this project of the Kingdom was not with Him like a politician's programme. It was a "Gospel." He knew it to be the will of God, and He believed it must come because the power of God was behind it. He had good news for men—even the good news that all this present reign of evil might and would end so soon as men turned to God and accepted His will. He knew that His own presence in the world was the beginning of the Kingdom; and He was Himself so constantly aware of the power of God that for Him it was a matter of immediate certainty that if only men would let God into their lives the building of the Kingdom was certain to follow. There was no hint of arrogance in His imperialism. "I can of mine own self do nothing" was a characteristic saying of His. He could preach the Gospel of the Kingdom only because He was a soul steeped in God. In that sense the message of Jesus was not either a political or a social message, but a religious message.

And yet it is very important to realize that this

Gospel which Jesus proclaimed does meet to the full
the demand which is so divinely strong in thousands
of hearts today—namely, the demand for a changed
world.   Thousands of young men and women are
positively impatient today when it is suggested to
them that they should be concerned about their own
souls.   They don't as yet care about their souls.
But they do care, and care intensely, about the
blatant evils of our day, and all those forces of
injustice in our world whereby millions of human
lives are thwarted, maimed, and spoilt.   The insistent challenge of the wrongs of men and women
who are chained and stunted by a cruel system of
industry, who are denied health and joy by the very
conditions of their lives, who are at times almost
maddened by impulses towards a fuller life which
can find no expression, who are crucified by a re-
lentless social order—that challenge bulks so much
more in many lives than any thought of personal
salvation, that the old evangelistic message about
the way to save one's soul is positively irritating to
some.   Thousands of such people are actually
annoyed and irritated by much that they hear in
churches.   It would seem to them a petty thing to
be worrying about their souls while men, women,
and little children are being so abused.   They think
conventional religion a selfish thing.   It might, of
course, be pointed out to such people that many
of the great evangelicals have also been among the
greatest of the servants of distressed humanity, and
that where evangelicalism is pure it creates public
spirited persons.   They will also probably find out

for themselves in time that if they are really to help they themselves must be changed. But to begin with, it is most important that we should realize that the message of Jesus was in its essence a message about the way to change the world. At the very beginning of His public ministry, He once expanded the Gospel of the Kingdom by uttering what modern language would call a manifesto. "The Spirit of the Lord is upon me: for he has consecrated me to preach the gospel to the poor, he has sent me to proclaim release for captives and recovery of sight for the blind, to set free the oppressed, to proclaim the Lord's year of favour" (Luke iv. 18-19, Moffatt's translation). All that was involved in the Gospel of the Kingdom of God. The designs of Jesus included all that the most tender heart could desire, and all that the boldest modern reformer could demand. What He lived for was to bring full life and full liberty to every child of God.

It was not in fact an individual salvation which He preached. He did not come simply to save individuals out of the world. He came to make certain a new heavens and a new earth. And the individual can never know the full joy of the Kingdom so long as there remains one soul outside it, or one evil custom which wounds human lives.

There are thousands of would-be reformers in the world today moved by sincere and holy passion. Yet most of them are ineffective, and many of them are hopelessly perplexed. What they need is a real leader with an inspired plan of action. They are waiting for some one to show them the real way forward. They are really waiting for Jesus though they may not know it. He alone can lead in this matter. He alone can show men how to get the power they need.

The Conditions of Entrance.—Let us ask, then, what Jesus has to say to any one who wants to help in bringing in the Kingdom. He expresses that by saying that they must first of all see the Kingdom themselves, or that they must enter it themselves; and when we ask what are the conditions of entrance we get a very astonishing answer.

"If any man will come after me let him deny himself and take up his cross daily. . . . He that loveth his life shall lose it, but he that loseth his life shall find it." "If any man come to me and hate not his father, and mother, and wife, and children and brethren and sisters, yea and his own life also, he cannot be my disciple."

This thought comes over and over again in His teaching. He demanded of men a surrender absolutely complete. He had no place in the band of His followers for the man who looked back, or who was willing to give only a part of himself. At the very threshold of the Kingdom stands this call for utter self-renunciation. For any man or woman who is thinking of dealing with Jesus, here is the first matter of vital moment. We must understand Him here or we shall go utterly wrong. What does He mean?

Surely He means just this—that if a man would enter the Kingdom his object in life must no longer be himself in any sense. He must no longer aim at his own advancement or his own profit. He must not live for his own career or his own comfort or his own fame and power. His purpose must cease to be his own establishment in ease or safety; he must be done with "getting on in life." And in place of these almost universal and extremely natural aims, he must put the one aim of helping the coming of the Kingdom of God. The selflessness which was so perfect in Himself He asks of all who would follow and help Him. Being a Christian is not something a man can add on to life. It cannot be one of many interests in a life. It can only be the one supreme and dominating thing. Perhaps no leader ever made such uncompromising demands of his followers.

No doubt, as they come to understand what He asked, many will say it is too much. "Why," they will say, "if we are thus to let go all our natural ambitions, and surrender the plans we have made for our lives—if we are no longer to try to get the things which we want to get, we might as well die." And Jesus does not dispute that view of the case. He deliberately says a man *must* die to enter the Kingdom, only He insists that such dying turns out to be in the long run the only real way into life —life full, and happy, and effective. It is not simply what we call sins which a man must surrender. It is his whole life so far as he has planned it for the advantage of self. Just as a soldier says, "I must serve my nation, and never mind what becomes of me," so a member of Christ's band must say, "I must serve the Kingdom, and never mind what becomes of myself." Sooner or later each man or woman who thus accepts Christ's terms will come to know what his or her "bit" must be. And if in the doing of that bit he or she should allow thoughts of self and ease to interfere with efficiency, then that man or woman is unworthy of Christ.

When this great transformation takes place in a man's life he is often said to be converted. And this is the only genuine and true form of conversion. Whatever spiritual experiences a man may have gone through, if he is not delivered from his self-regarding impulses, then he is not converted to the Christian position. About this point it is well that we should all be perfectly clear. We may refuse to think seriously of any such surrender of self. We may hold it absurd that anything so extreme should be asked. We may point blank refuse. But we cannot explain away the fact that that *is* what Christ asks. We may take it or leave it, but we cannot be Christians on any other terms.

The End of Ordinary Ambitions.—And now let us notice what will happen so soon as the great surrender has been achieved. The first result is that the ordinary ambitions which excite and embitter men are cut at the root. The love of money, the love of power, the love of status, the desire to override other men, one and all wither so soon as a man has become delivered from self. A man will, of course, always need sustenance for himself and his family. As Jesus put it, "Our Heavenly Father knoweth that we have need of such things." But in a just world that sustenance will always be secure to any honest servant, and the eye of a disciple will not be fixed upon that, but upon the service he can render humanity; or in other words, upon what he can do to bring in the Kingdom. There may seem sometimes to be little outward difference between two busy business or professional men, one of whom is working for money, and the other of whom is working for society. But morally they are poles apart. They hardly belong to the same world. The difference between their spiritual attitudes is enormous.

So soon, however, as the ordinary ambitions are exorcised from the spirit of man, wonderful consequences appear. It turns out that in that way the giant evils of the world receive a death blow. Consider such familiar evils as sweating, overwork, bad housing, and congested urban areas. The real root from which all these giant social weeds have grown is the root of avarice. Because some one, somewhere, and at some point was over-anxious to make money these things appeared. In each case some one has considered personal money gain before the rights of other individuals. Some one has been trying to get too much work for the wage he paid, or to put too many people to live on the land he was going to let, or to give too little in healthy house room for the rent he was going to charge. But in a society where the members had been brought to put the common good before personal gain, none of these things could occur. A servant of the Kingdom would rather be *very* poor himself, than take the life energy of another on starvation terms.

Or, again, consider war. The real cause whence come wars is often just the same lust after gold. It is this which sets rival nations by the ears. They come into conflict often over matters concerned with commercial gain. They clash because they want to override each other and not to serve each other. Or it may be that they clash because they are alike animated by the lust for power—because they have made a national policy of the impulse to dominate others. And so long as there are in one world two nations pursuing that policy, war with its horrors is an inevitable result. But so soon as men put service before self the lust for power dies an inevitable death. No man lusting after power can live on terms of sympathy with Jesus. All who enter His Kingdom on His terms become at once forces that tend to prevent wars.

Or, consider, again, a more personal evil— namely impurity. It has played havoc with every civilization, and has been ravaging ours of late. And its roots lie in the same instinct that makes a man put self-gratification before consideration for others. The man who takes her all from a woman without giving his all in return, or the woman who tempts a man to the loss of his chastity, is really consenting to use another personality as the mere instrument of pleasure, and taking what he or she holds to be gain at the expense of loss to others. Such action is rooted in a self-regard from which a surrendered spirit is for ever free. No man whose life interest is an interest in service can possibly traffic in such pleasures. A world without prostitution in it would be so infinitely healthier, happier, and more wholesome than this world, that many hold it to be an impossibility. But it comes definitely nearer with every man who enters the Kingdom on Christ's terms, and will come into complete being so soon as the race becomes wise enough to recognize Jesus as the Lord of Life. I might easily go on to speak of other evils, but it is unnecessary. Any one who thinks will find that a Kingdom based upon the self-surrender of all its citizens would be a Kingdom from which all the old familiar evils of the world would disappear.

I have no sympathy with those who on supposedly Christian grounds disparage efforts to secure legislation to end sweating, or to secure good houses for all, or to protect girls and to restrain the sensualist. It is quite possible that in a new sense the law (or in this case laws) may prove a schoolmaster to bring us to Christ. But I do think it very well worth while that we should pause here just for a moment to realize that the one really effective way of dealing with all the world's evils, is the way of Jesus. You may induce a man to believe many doctrines, and still he may go on fostering social evils and profiting by them. You may induce men to join organized churches, and afterwards find them very busy in profiteering, and in commercial oppression. But when a man enters the Kingdom of God on the terms made plain by Christ, all that ends at once. He has no further interest in self-

assertion. He becomes at once a force for the pro-
tection and help of others. Kingdom Christianity
is the sole real remedy for social, national, and
international evils.

Self-Surrender Is Not Life-Surrender.—Having
looked squarely at the first demand of Jesus, for
utter self-surrender, it becomes immediately most
important to realize that there was involved in it
no tendency towards narrow living, or any of that
suspicious attitude towards a full life which is common in many religious circles. We shall not get at
the real purpose of Jesus until we put side by side
His call for self-surrender, and His declaration, "I
am come that ye might have life, and that ye might
have it more abundantly." It was indeed just life
that Jesus wanted to give men. To His vision their
actual life was a poor and mean affair—a sorry
scrambling amidst things of little worth, while the
real wealth of existence of which they were capable
was unrealized. They were scraping in the dust
for gold, wallowing in a surfeit of sense pleasures,
and trampling on each other in the process, while
all the while He knew they might one and all have
been living full and free lives, in touch with beauty,
and tuned to divine harmonies.

No one can read Christ's life honestly and make
any mistake about His interest in whatever was
normal and wholesome in human life. He knew
all about the lives of farmers, and fishermen, and
traders. He was interested in family life, and
marriage, and felt to the full the charm of children.
He enjoyed Himself in the society of full-blooded,

warm-hearted people. He had plainly worshipped the Father much by reading in the book of nature. He was most at home in the open clean country. He had marked the beauty of flowers, felt the wonder of the mystery of growth, and enjoyed the sunshine and the rain. He was of the family of all those for whom this wonderful, many-sided, varied, and splendid thing which we call life is a source of unending joy and fascination. There is something cold and forbidding in all asceticism. It involves always a covert reproach to Him who designed our humanity. He would, indeed, be a strange God who should first make man capable of a thousand varied activities and then call upon him to exercise only two or three of them. But Jesus was so wholly free from asceticism that those who had not understood Him actually reproached Him as a gluttonous man and a wine-bibber. He was too great to be a John the Baptist who was at home in the desert. Jesus could only be at home in the midst of ordinary many-sided life.

What, then, of this call to self-denial! Well, it was a call to self-surrender, but not a call to world renunciation. Men and women were to go on living in the world, and were to continue to exercise their gifts and talents there, only all now with a new motive. They were to be busy not for self but for all men. The statesman was to be busy, not that he might rise to some supreme place of power, but that national affairs might be well administered. The fisherman was to catch fish, not that he might make a corner in the fish market and so become

rich, but that the people might have fresh and
wholesome food. The bootmaker was to work
hard, not for the utmost possible profit, but that the
rest of men might have the best possible boots at
the cheapest possible price. The trader was to go
on with his business and put all his brains into it,
not that he might make a pile and retire early into
idleness, but that he might help the free exchange of
the world's goods, and bring ease to lives that were
straitened. The musician was to go on making
music, and the best music he could—not for the
highest possible fees, but that he might bring a
worthy joy into the greatest possible number of
lives. The physician was to be busier than ever,
but with a passion for health, and not with a
covetous eye on guineas. In fact, the self-regarding element was to pass out of every life, and so
each life was to be set free to become something
finer and larger and happier. He *was* giving men
the secret of life, when He called them to give it up.
It does in literal fact turn out to be true, that he who
loseth his life shall find it, and none but those who
have so lost life can ever imagine what a great and
satisfying and romantic thing life may be through
all its course.

It was this that He was thinking of when He
uttered His well-known promise: "All things shall
be added unto you." So they are in literal fact.
And the truly wealthy man—the man who has truly
found well being—is always a man who has first
laid down his life and all his selfish ambitions.

CHAPTER III

FURTHER FEATURES OF THE KINGDOM

WE shall get further light on the nature of the Kingdom of God, if we now approach it from a different angle. It is a Kingdom in which men have not only got rid of self-regard, but in which they take seriously the brotherhood of man. The phrase which Jesus instinctively used to describe another man was always "Thy brother." It was for Him one and the same thing to teach men that God was their Father and to teach that all of them were brethren. His own attitude was really well described by saying, "He was not ashamed to call them brethren."

But while it is the case that the two truths—the Fatherhood of God, and the brotherhood of man—are really one and the same truth looked at from different sides, it is *not* true that men inevitably receive them together. It is a congenial thing to most people to believe that God is their Father, and often it is a very uncongenial thing to believe that all other men are their brethren. It is possible to have a great deal of emotional pleasure in the fact that we have a Father in heaven who loves us, and yet at the same time to deny in thought and action our brotherhood with other classes and races than our own.

The brotherhood of man in fact turns out to be of all truths the most revolutionary, and for the drastic changes which would come with its recognition many devout persons are not at all ready. For the Jews of Christ's time mankind consisted of two utterly different groups—Jews, who were the favoured of God, and Gentiles, who were outsiders. For the Greeks the two groups were Greeks, and all the others—comprehensively labelled "barbarians." For Romans, the groups were Roman citizens, and the rest. Further, all over the world men were divided into the free and the slaves, and so different was the status of the two groups that they were hardly held to be all alike human. Within the Jewish state there were the Scribes and Pharisees, and "the people" often called "accurst." When Jesus called on men to believe in the brotherhood of man, He was asking the race to be done with these artificial distinctions. And in so far as the world understood Him it simply gasped, and then dismissed Him as a dreamer.

That is what men have done ever since even in the countries called Christian. Most of us still believe, not by any deliberate mental process, but by inherited instinct, in numberless race and class distinctions which deny brotherhood. There are British people, and "foreigners" for whom we are a little sorry. There are white men, and black men whose destiny it is to be ruled by the whites and who are hardly in the same sense human. There are county families and the "other people," most of whom, poor souls, are "rather bounders." There are professional men, and tradesmen, "many of them, you know, wonderfully decent chaps!" There are "the best people," who often cling to the title in spite of a minimum outfit of morals; and there are "the others" to whom one need hardly be polite. There are Church folk who have on them the hall mark of an aristocratic institution, and Dissenters who are so ignorant and demonstrative even in their religion. There are skilled tradesmen, and common labourers, who are often treated as scum. There are the respectable, and the fallen—the well-to-do, and the failures—the people in society, and the people outside of it—the educated who are sometimes educated in most things except true courtesy, and the ignorant—gentlemen, and bounders—ladies, and "women"—public school men, and all the rest—"bloods," and commoners, etc., through all the vast list of human social vagaries which must so amuse and weary our patient and generous common Father.

Now when Jesus announced the Kingdom of God He was really saying, "Let us be done once and for all with all these follies, some of which are cruel, and all of which are based upon a lie." "All ye are brethren," He said, and it follows that the true life of mankind can only be based upon a full and generous recognition of the fact. Those who would enter the Kingdom must be prepared to let go their race prejudices, and their social prejudices, and all their familiar and inherited forms of pride. Many of us will have to be born again, and born different, before that will be possible with us; but then, as we have seen, a man who enters the Kingdom must be born again. Patronage will not meet the demand made of us here. Neither will philanthropy. You do not patronize a brother or deal with him by way of charity. You treat him as one of the family, and share your life with him. Nothing short of that will satisfy Christ's demands. You are to give your brother not your money or your pity, but yourself. You are to learn to the full the art of brotherhood towards him.

And this as we begin to be serious with it turns out to involve a multitude of things that used to seem unheard of. If all men are my brothers, then I must be content to let my life become involved with theirs. I cannot isolate myself either from their sorrows or their wrongs. What hurts them must hurt me. I cannot enjoy security while they are insecure, nor comfort and plenty while they are in pain and need.

Vast vistas open up here which can really only be touched on in the slightest way at this point. It is here in fact that the social and political implicates of living according to the principles of the Kingdom begin to appear. Let me indicate only a few.

Industry.—There is at present in being nearly all over the world a system of industry according to which the many are exploited for the gain of the few. Under that system the wage-earner sells his

labour for as much as he can get, and thereafter
has very little control over his life. He works at
another's bidding and for another's profit. Within
the factory, or yard, or shop where he labours his
place is very nearly that of a machine. No call is
made upon him for the exercise of many of his
finer powers. He does not hold a responsible office.
His life is one of mechanical routine which tends
actually to dull and impair the soul. Even when
he is neither overworked nor underpaid, he is not
given a status which corresponds with his true
dignity as a son of God. In that industrial world
he is not a citizen but a convenience. That is really
why all over the world the men in the ranks of
labour are in revolt. Their immediate demands
may at times seem unreasonable. The reasons they
give for their violent tactics may seem insufficient.
But below all that heaving mass of discontent what
is really happening is just that men made in the
image of God are in revolt against a system that
denies them the opportunity of a full human life.
The explanation of labour unrest is really souls in
revolt. Now no citizen of the Kingdom can accept
such a system for his brethren. He may not know
how exactly it is to be changed, nor what different
organization of industry is to supersede it. But a
system that does such despite to his brethren he
cannot accept. Kingdom Christianity demands
something drastically different.

Housing.—In exactly the same way the citizen
of the Kingdom will find himself involved in the
housing question. The houses in which a vast

number of people live in this country are such as to deprive them of the possibility of a full human life. They are fatal to real health, fatal to quiet, almost fatal to cleanliness. They make a mother's task too hard for even the strongest of women. They rob fathers of a real resting place in the evenings. They provide no opportunity of social intercourse for the young. In many cases they make even decency cruelly difficult. Christ's people cannot accept them for any portion of God's family. Building the Kingdom must mean rebuilding a vast proportion of the houses of Great Britain.

Education.—Equally inevitable is it that disciples of Christ will find themselves bound over to an interest in the matter of education. Christ's own aim for men and for *all* men was fullness of life. And fullness of life means adequate education. Not such education as we have at present, which tends to deal with children in crowds and so to impose one pattern on their plastic natures, but an education which shall really draw out all the latent powers in each personality, and so introduce them to real life.

Health.—So also in the matter of health. Full life means health. All that destroys health is destroying the human careers of men and women. A disciple of the Kingdom will therefore find himself compelled to accept the challenge of whatsoever destroys health. He will be concerned not only with remedial measures such as hospitals. He will care about town planning, and the national supply of water and good food. He will not think the smoke nuisance a little thing.   He will probably come to think the drink evil a monstrous thing.   At point after point he will find himself constrained to be a rebel against things as they are.   It may well turn out that he can only touch the evils which confront him at some one point, and that only in a very partial and half-successful way.   But he will have a heart in sympathy with all everywhere who are putting forth devoted hands to set his brethren free from anything that now hampers their life.

Amusements.—And here a thought about amusements may well be expressed.   I conceive that a man who really cares about his brethren will wish that they should have that amount of pure amusement which our human constitution demands.   But he will not wish to see any man or any woman set to perform a task for the amusement of others which he would not be willing to perform himself. In general, he will not consent to pay any man to do *anything* which he would not be willing to do himself.   And the particular application of that thought to amusements is that he will not pay to see any one do anything which he could not do himself without loss of dignity or self-respect.

Inequalities of Income.—Behind these a still more difficult question insists upon obtruding itself. Will a man who really lives out a belief in brotherhood find that he can accept the inequalities of income which are such a glaring feature of our present social and economic order?   Probably most people will answer "No!   We must work for such a readjustment as shall give to all men and women

at least a chance of real self-realization, and to that
end we must see to it that the fruits of civilization
are at least more equally divided." Perhaps that is
all the answer that need be suggested here. The
members of the Kingdom are all of them people
who have escaped from any avaricious desire to
make money: if they find themselves in a higher
degree of comfort than is possible to the majority
just now, they may satisfy themselves by making
sure that they use their comfort to increase their
efficiency and not to clog their energies. It may
be enough to meet the demand of Christ if they
watch with vigilance lest any undue desire to keep
what they have got should affect their thinking
about political and social issues, or their conduct in
life's affairs generally. Christ never said dogmatically that His followers *must* be poor. He only
implied in all that He said that they must be willing
to be poor, if in that way they can help the coming
of the Kingdom. There is no necessary virtue in a
meagre manner of existence, and sordid ways of
living always lessen the real value of life. It is
even quite possible that a man might lose some of
his power to lift by first going down voluntarily to
that low level of material existence from which he
wishes to raise all men. Perhaps in this connection
the real question a man must face is whether he is
using his advantages merely for self, or for the
cause of the Kingdom.

And yet when all this has been said, there will,
I think, always remain some who are not satisfied—
some who are troubled by incomes of £500 a year

and upwards, even though they be well earned. They will not suggest that there is anything wrong in such an income itself.   They may even wish that all men could have £1000 a year.   But they will question the reality of their brotherly spirit so long as they themselves have so much more than the majority of their brethren.   Some of them will accept voluntary poverty with all its disadvantages just in order that they may get nearer to their brethren.   And it may well be that there is a great part to be played in bringing in the Kingdom by such people.   The Kingdom is not based upon material poverty, but just because it is very hard to build, it may well be that those who have become poor for Christ's sake will alone have power for some of the specially hard parts of the work.

Coloured Races.—Passing from that difficult point we must stay a moment to realize what brotherhood means in relation to the races of Asia and Africa.   Few dividing walls prove so strong and high as the colour wall.   Not a few good and generous souls have found themselves unable to subdue a certain obstinate instinct of distaste when brought into intimate contact with people on the other side of that wall.   Easterns probably have that experience in relation to Westerns, and many Westerns have it in their turn.   The instinctive attitude of the efficient Briton towards such people is apt to be at best one of kindly domination.   He does not really feel that Chinese, Indians, and Africans belong to the same race as himself.   He can bear with them so long as they are merely labourers. When they aspire to share the professions, or to cooperate in government, he is apt to be indignant. In fact, it is rooted in his very being that such people are not his equals and never can be.

But when Christ said that God is the Father of all men, He meant *all* men. When He called on those who would follow Him to recognize others as their brethren, He made no exception in the case of coloured men. When He forbade us to call any man common or unclean, He was laying down an absolute rule. When He commissioned His people to preach the Gospel to every creature, He meant that the Gospel is true for every creature, and it is part of that Gospel to tell men that they are all one great family—the family of the sons of God.

Here indeed is a hard matter for either an Englishman or a Scot. Though he may have felt drawn to Christ, he is apt to pause when he begins to realize that this Jesus who does in some mysterious way to touch the deepest chords of his being, has yet such strange and almost fantastic things to suggest to him. Yes! a man might well be inwardly moved to do much for Christ, and yet feel that to recognize coloured men as even potential equals is altogether too much. Truly it is a hard thing to accept the principles of the Kingdom, and to enter it as a whole-hearted citizen. But Jesus never compromises. He identifies Himself with the least of His brethren. If we will not accept these least, we may not accept Him. Here is another thing which we may take or leave, but which we can by no possibility explain away.

It is a plain matter of honesty that at this point we should discriminate.

We are apt to talk easily about the backward races, and to include under that title all but the white races. But it is certain that there are important respects in which we Westerns have much to learn from Asiatics. It may well be that the contemplative Hindu, who sits so lightly to material things, is far nearer to the pattern of Christ than the bustling commercial man of the West. The distinctive Christian graces are "love, joy, peace, longsuffering, gentleness, goodness, faith, meekness, temperance." And many who know the East tell us that it is there that those graces flourish most naturally. It is far from the truth to imagine that we Westerns will never have to sit at the feet of the Easterns in the attitude of scholars.

On the other hand, of course, it is true that the members of some coloured races are still our backward brothers. And though we may look forward eagerly to the day when they will be our grown-up brothers, we cannot treat them as what they are not. To learn the right way of dealing with them is something which can only be achieved by a great deal of true feeling and inspired tact. It is very bad for a little brother to treat him as if he were grown up: to lend him a gun, for instance, which he cannot manage, or to offer him tobacco for which his body is not ready. And so it would be more than bad for some of our backward brethren to treat them in all things as we treat one another. It might be actually cruel. To impose upon African natives tasks of self-government which are utterly beyond them might be to plunge them into the miseries of anarchy. To encourage marriages between black and white while the two races are at such very different stages of moral and intellectual development might mean only preparing misery for those involved in such marriages. To realize our brotherhood with them fully may prove a long and difficult affair. It will be necessary that many members of the Kingdom should give themselves to careful and detailed study of that part of the work. A hundred difficulties will present themselves which only patience and a great deal of large-hearted wisdom can overcome. And it is work which can be done only by those who believe with Jesus that these backward brethren *are* our brethren. It can be done only by those who *want* in the end to achieve full and generous equality with them. We are on the whole a little further on than they are. Not so very far, for the brute and the savage sometimes rear their heads even in our decent British life. Yet still we are further on. We are like older brothers to them. We might do for them just what generous older brothers can do for the youngsters in a family. We might help them to become men. But only if we share Christ's faith about them—only if we believe that in the deepest truth of things all men *are* brethren.

Internationalism.—And now let us consider just one last consequence of an honest belief in this brotherhood. Jesus announced the coming of the Kingdom of God, but only of one Kingdom. He did not suggest that there should be a British Kingdom, and an American Kingdom, and a German Kingdom—but one Kingdom which should cover the whole earth. That is to say, He rose in His thinking above all national barriers. It was an amazing thing for a Jew to do, for among the Jews the consciousness of nationality was extraordinarily acute. Yet for Him the Kingdom meant something that was above and beyond national distinctions. One essential glory of that Kingdom lay in this, that its coming meant the achievement of the unity of mankind. It was for Him something into which all nations might enter, and in which all would find a harmonious life greater and richer than they had ever known in their isolation. Into it indeed each nation was to bring its glory and honour. To its ultimate wealth and beauty each would have something to contribute. They were not to be called upon to surrender their peculiar gifts or to abandon their own special genius, but they were to find for them a fuller and a greater exercise when they came to live in relations of unity with all other peoples. It is here that we come into sight of the full splendour and magnificence of the Kingdom. It is to be something far more adequate to our loftiest dreams than any partial empire, or any empire dominated by the genius of one people could possibly be. At this point Jesus becomes the loftiest and the most imperially minded of all the world's thinkers. Nothing less could satisfy that great heart of His and that masterly mind than a unified life for all the peoples of the world, expressed in mutual service and a generous regard for each other's freedom.

And this for a servant of the Kingdom today has immediate and far-reaching consequences. It means that he must regard it as a thing intolerable that the nations of the world should remain in relations of antagonism, rivalry, and mutual suspicion. He cannot be merely a patriot, however truly he may love his own people. He *must* in spirit stretch out hands to all other nations and desire relations of brotherhood with them. He must be an agent for reconciliation. He must hate wars, as the very negation of all that he holds most dear. He must long to be delivered from his own national prejudices, and honestly want to be friends with God's other children of all kinds. Otherwise he is not of the Kingdom at all.

Here, again, no doubt a host of practical and complicated difficulties confront Christ's people. There stand in the way of the realization of their ideas uncounted political tangles, and a cloud of poisonous passions—the aftermath of wars, tumults, oppressions, and the past follies of statesmen. The story of the crimes committed against our common brotherhood in the lifetime of this generation is past all telling. Europe today stinks and reeks with the odour of follies and brutalities which have degraded our common humanity, and left the peoples sore, angry, and ashamed. The outlook for the apostles of internationalism is as dark as it ever was. And yet at least it has been shown beyond all contradiction that nothing but internationalism will

ever make the life of the human race a noble or
even a tolerable thing. At last we know the worst
about every other conception. At last we are beginning to see that if the whole enterprise of humanity
on this little globe is not to end in shame and defeat
we must learn how to achieve brotherhood. At last
all current history is calling in loud and tragic tones
for that which apostles of the Kingdom can alone
bring to pass. The work those apostles are called
on to do is difficult indeed; but it is that or utter
and final shame. And in that sense this is indeed a
great day for any man or woman who can be bold
and desperate enough to abandon his or her life
to utter obedience to the thought of Jesus. He
must reign or nobody will reign. He must become
Lord of all the earth, or base passions will destroy
the house of civilization which we have built. It
is, to paraphrase a well-known phrase, "The Kingdom or Hell." Here indeed is a call to all who
can be great in spirit. Here is all that men great
in heart or head could possibly ask of adventure
and great business. The only real question about
the Kingdom is whether any of us can ever be
great enough to belong to it.

From these far-reaching thoughts, it may be
well to turn for a moment to our actual daily life.
The real problem of brotherhood for most of us
is not the problem of treating either dark people or
Germans in a Christian way, but the problem of
being Christian to the ordinary and actual people
whom we meet in our daily lives—the people in our
own families, the other men or women in our year,

the dons and tutors of our colleges, the queer and
odd people who appear on the scene for us while
life's wheel spins us about. It is they who are
going to test us all and demonstrate whether we
have an honest right to talk about brotherhood.
Never having been in the East I find it quite easy
to be positively thrilled by the idea of being
"awfully decent" to black people. As no Germans
of the blatant Prussian type come into my present
world, it costs me nothing to agree that we ought
to achieve relations of reconciliation with them.
But there are people in my present world who
present just as tough a problem as any swaggering
junker could. They are the people who are really
going to test me if I aspire to belong to the Kingdom. Something of the same sort is true for every
man. What of that cheeky little beggar you know,
who is just as cocksure and aggressive as a quarter
of an education ever made any man! What of that
terribly religious person whose whining voice seems
to go down your spine and make you shudder!
What of that young fool who is always telling filthy
yarns so that you hear the fellows round him laughing the silly half-ashamed laughter which blue
stories always produce! What of that rich and
well-born person who passes you by as if you had
hardly any right to exist on the same globe as himself! What of those chaps in your college whom
you feel to be bounders! What of that unattractive
girl you come across who is left alone by most
people and must feel horribly lonely! What of
conceited dons, tyrannous seniors, cheeky juniors,

bullying professors, and fussy mistresses! What of your gyp, your landlady, those business chaps you sometimes meet, or those shop girls you come across at times! If you want to enter the Kingdom you must believe concerning them all that they are your brothers and sisters. Your creed will have to express itself in action or it will remain only an insincere sentiment—and it is insincere sentiments that have made the Church a laughing stock in so many quarters.

It must surely be becoming plain that to believe in brotherhood is likely to turn out a matter so difficult that to achieve it will involve a great career. But it will turn out to be more than difficult. It will at times involve agony. It is very easy to *talk* about fellowship. It sounds as if it would be something very jolly, like having a good time among friends. But fellowship or brotherhood has another side to it. There will be times when your brothers fall into sorrow, and unless you are going to desert them you will have to share their sorrow. They will have big worries in their lives and you will have to share those worries. Worse still they will do vile and weak things sometime which will disgust you, and you will have to choose between leaving them in the time of their greatest need, or staying in fellowship with them at the price of sharing their shame, and being dragged by them into a wrestle with evil which will strain your very heart. It was so with Jesus. The men and women with whom He lived in fellowship exacted from Him the last farthing which fellowship can ever involve. They so sinned that they would have broken His heart had it not been a heart strong with the strength of God. They flung shame and disappointment, and loneliness and agony upon Him, as if unconsciously they were determined to see how much He could stand, and whether suffering could break His love. They resisted Him and flouted Him and tried to trample upon Him, till at last He saw there was only one way in which to do the best for them, and that was to die at their hands. He could not overcome them in the interchange of ordinary life. He taught, and pled, and served, and loved, but all these things together did not succeed. There was ultimately but one way left open to Him, and that the way of the cross. In this supreme matter He found once more that the only way to live was to die. And His brotherhood stood the strain. He would not desert His brethren even when the price of holding to His love was that dreadful price. He would go to Gethsemane and Golgotha, if in that way He might at last win His brethren. And it was in that way He came to His victory. It has been the fact of Christ's agony unto death that has broken down human opposition and turned men from the sins which destroy life. He saved us by fellowship indeed, but it had to be fellowship unto death. He believed in brotherhood, but He had to prove it by dying at the hands of His brethren. And the same thing must always hold for us.

Put the thing, if you like, in the most colloquial words possible—say that after all being a Christian simply consists in being decent to other chaps and not in believing things or in going to churches. Well, if you really mean it you will find that "being decent to other chaps" means sticking by them in their troubles, even when they have made utter fools of themselves. It will mean allowing their needs to interfere with your leisure and your pleasure. It may even mean having to give up some of your plans in life, and having your own affairs hopelessly compromised. You will find that being decent to other chaps is going to take a terrific toll from you. You will never find you have come to a point when you can say to your brother, "What have I to do with you?" and that brother's needs may cling about you till you are hardly a free man. And then, though you despise theology and scoff at orthodoxy, you will have discovered for yourself that man's redemption can only be achieved by the cross, and that only a suffering God could save you or anybody else.

Probably most of us are susceptible to the fascination of the idea of the Kingdom of God. Imagination and heart catch fire at this conception of one world-wide Kingdom of peace, wherein men attain to their fullest possible life. But it would be well that before we go any further we should reckon also with the fact that that Kingdom can only be built by suffering, and that brotherhood is an impossible thing to those who will not carry a cross for the sake of their brethren. The Kingdom was founded upon an agony and bloody sweat. The cross is its eternal symbol. He who would march with Jesus must march under that banner.

CHAPTER IV

METHODS IN THE KINGDOM

IT is not difficult to commend the Kingdom of God to the men and women of Britain so long as only some of its features are insisted on.

There is a certain obvious fascination in the idea of complete and utter self-abnegation. It is a conception that links itself up with all that was finest in the old aristocratic ideal. The young knight of old was trained to believe that he must never hold his own life dear unto himself when any knightly cause was concerned. The finest of the old families of the country still hold that they were born to serve, and that self must not be allowed to interfere with their service. Our soldiers never become true soldiers until in spirit they have laid down their lives, and they know by experience the wonder of that joy which comes to the man who has got beyond self-regard. Wherever good sportsmen are to be found there it is certain that the call to risk everything in a great cause will find a response that springs from the deep places in human nature.

Further, the whole conception of a new and well-ordered world is certain to appeal to all who have been touched in heart by the miseries and injustices of our present world. Enormous numbers of men and women are heartily ashamed of our present life in many of its aspects. Our old ways are realized to be quite unworthy of a nation whose present liberty has been bought by the blood of heroes. It is this that lies behind the present passion for reconstruction. And if Jesus can show us the way to a new and better world, that would decide the question of His claims for thousands.

Again, all that is really pure and noble in radicalism tends to enlist men on Christ's side. Radicalism may seem at times to be merely an ugly form of class selfishness. But radicalism at its best is really the result of a passionate revolt of heart and conscience against a world that has been distorted by aggressive selfishness until much that is in it constitutes an affront to the Creator. And to radicals of that quality Jesus has always seemed to be a kindred spirit. In the halls of some of the most revolutionary and anti-clerical groups in Europe the portrait of Christ is none the less hung up as an object for reverence.

In other words, wherever men of any kind have any unselfish idealism within them there the conception of the Kingdom of God has power over their minds and enlists their sympathies.

But it would be well, before we go any further, to face the fact that there are features of the Kingdom of God as Jesus preached it, which do not appeal to the average Englishman, and perhaps even less to the average Scot.

1. To begin with, there is a large group of

sayings in the gospels which might be summed up in the familiar words, *"Blessed are the meek*, for they shall inherit the earth."   Now meekness is one of those virtues which most men admire in others, but which very few men desire for themselves.   It is a convenient thing to find others meek; but most of us believe it might turn out a very unpleasant thing to *be* meek.   Probably most men regard it in their hearts as a most excellent quality for women to have, and otherwise associate it with those admirable and pious youths whose goodness is intimately related to their lack of high vitality.

Now no doubt this is partly due to sheer misunderstanding of what Christian meekness really means.   We think of it as rather a weak thing— as due in part at least to lack of proper spirit.   But it cannot be that.   It is a quality which Christ had. And no man who has ever looked at the real Jesus could possibly suspect Him of want of high vitality, strength, and courage.

As a matter of fact, it is the opposite of self-assertiveness, and is therefore a strong man's quality.   Christian meekness means that a man has attained to such a perfection of self-control that he will refuse to assert self even under great provocation.   To weak men pride, anger, and quick resentment come easily.   He must be very strong who would be meek as Christ was meek.   Yet even so, it is hard to want to be meek. It does involve humility.   And humility is another quality which we approve, but do not as a rule desire.   We have seen that we are to deny self, if we would enter the

Kingdom, and for many men the denial of personal pride is the hardest part of it all. They can easily deny the flesh the pleasures it craves, but to deny the spirit is a far harder thing.

We may want the Kingdom, but most of us would like to be allowed to fight for it. We would like to be allowed to express our reforming zeal by the forcible crushing of opposition, and by coercing those who will not agree. Crusading of the old mediæval type appeals to us. The men who cried out for short sharp work with infidels and all pagan opponents would still rouse an echo in our hearts. But Christ will not meet us here. "My Kingdom is not a worldly Kingdom, else would My servants fight." "Put up thy sword." Mere force cannot achieve Christ's ends. It is a thing irrelevant to His real purposes. Men have tried all down the centuries to carve out a Christian civilization with the power of the sword. They have patently failed. And the reason is that they have tried an impossible method. No doubt the vast majority of Christ's loyal followers hold that force must at times be met by force. Reluctantly but with clear conscience they justify defensive warfare. That, however, leaves the main position quite clear. Force may restrain the evil-doer, but it cannot build the Kingdom. It is not a constructive power. It is not to the fighting instinct that Christ appeals. He needs men with many of a soldier's qualities: the power to take huge risks with a laugh, personal courage, loyalty to comrades, discipline, endurance, and so on. But for the will to dominate others by mere force He has no use. For the touchy, proud, or arrogant spirit there is no place in His army.

2. A second feature that is hard to accept is *Christ's law of forgiveness.* Prof. Seeley declares it to have been His greatest moral innovation. His followers are not to deal in retaliation. The old law had said, "Eye for eye, tooth for tooth, hand for hand, foot for foot, burning for burning, wound for wound, stripe for stripe." That is still exactly the conception of justice which dominates the minds of the majority of men. But Christ calls His men and women to imitate that spirit which led Him when faced by His own cruel and lawless murderers to pray, "Father forgive them."

It is certainly not natural. Our natural instinct rather agrees with Cicero, who accounted that man happy who on his deathbed could say that no man had done more good to his friends, or more harm to his enemies. Christ, on the other hand, would account that man happy who had most generously and freely forgiven his enemies. And He made His demand absolute. He would hear of no limitations. To one of His disciples, who had stretched his spirit to the point at which he thought it might be right to continue this policy until seven times, Christ replied by saying, "No, but unto seventy times seven." The world of that day gasped at such a doctrine. And it still does so. It is almost universally held that such forgiveness is sure to be interpreted as a sign of weakness. The refusal of it has been justified of late a thousand times on just that ground. But forgiveness—real forgiveness, and not merely a cowardly refusal to display resentment—involves great strength. Aristotle, in drawing the picture of that high-minded man whom he accepted as his moral ideal, declared that he would be too great to notice small offences, and would pass them by in sheer pride, while for great offences he would take a truly great revenge. But Christ, with a far deeper moral insight, declared that real greatness of mind would show itself in a forgiveness which would never fail. He had climbed to heights undreamt of even by that great Greek moralist, when He prayed, "Father forgive them."

The secret of Christ's demand lies in the fact that forgiveness is the only ultimately successful way of overcoming evil. It is so, to begin with, in the case of individuals. Threats and punishments fail to eradicate the evil in man. At best they only force it underground. Bribes and promises fail to produce the virtuous heart. Their ultimate appeal is to the greed in man. Evil is a stronger thing than either the fear of pain or the hope of future reward. But it is *not* stronger than forgiving love. Jesus used that weapon with the Magdalene, with the thief on the cross, with Peter, and with Zacchæus. And in all these cases it achieved the great result. It is the one weapon which God puts into the hands of men wherewith they can make headway against evil. Some evils which society has never managed to control, are just evils which society has never forgiven. Further, the same truth holds in connection with groups of men —with families, clans, classes, and nations. So long

as such groups act on the principle of retaliation one
act of violence leads to another in an endless and
tragic chain. Thus come vendettas, family feuds,
class wars, and international wars. Politics and
diplomacy, which disregard Christ, holding Him an
unpractical dreamer, have proved powerless to
break these dire traditions of evil. Some of them
have for centuries overshadowed the life of whole
nations.

One thing alone can deliver the world, and usher
in a new day for mankind. And that one thing is
forgiveness. It ends evil because it wins the evil-
doer. It gets at the root of evil, and undermines
the spirit that produces strife. It saves the sinner
because it makes its appeal to the good that is in
him, and calls it into life. In individual cases it
may seem to fail, but for all that it is for the race
the supreme secret of escape from evil. Therefore
Christ made it one of the fundamentals of His
Kingdom.

3. A third point suggests itself here. I can
perhaps express it by saying that *the Kingdom cannot be organized into existence.* It does not come
with an outward show. Organization is, of course,
essential to all well-ordered life. It is an inevitable
thing among intelligent and civilized people. But
it is not a creative force. It directs life, and does
not produce it. It cannot create the spirit of the
Kingdom, and until the spirit is there no amount of
organization can set up that Kingdom.

Nowadays we tend to have a strange faith in
organization. We seem to have an instinct for

propaganda, monster meetings, and magnificent manifestos. We create leagues and federations, with officials, constitutions, and funds (that always seem inadequate). We canvass for members, until many people could not say how many such societies they belong to. The roads of progress seem positively congested by them. We have prevention societies organized over against almost every known evil. And yet the strongholds of evil do not seem greatly disturbed.

Jesus seems to have been quite uninterested in such things. He created almost no organization. He seemed suspicious of all outward show. He said His Kingdom would grow as seeds grow—that the spirit of it would work as leaven works—that it would spread like an infection. It begins to come into being so soon as men anywhere catch the spirit of it. It takes outward form so soon as the inward reality is there. But funds and fuss, and demonstrations and canvassings, do not bring it nearer. "He did not strive nor cry."

No doubt as it grows the Kingdom will transform politics and governments. It will inevitably and drastically reconstruct industry and commerce. It will end armies and navies. It will revolutionize education. It does mean a new heaven and a new earth. And no doubt, too, its servants will have to accept such callings as politics, and give themselves to the business and the theory of government. The Kingdom is not something in the air. It is tremendously and blessedly real. God forbid that I should do anything but thank Him for the labours of all who are trying to lay hands on the tangled affairs of this world and bend them to the pattern of Christ. I conceive that such things as housing reform, educational reform, temperance reform, poor law reform, and so on, lie in the very forefront of the labours to which servants of the Kingdom are committed. Shaftesbury, Octavia Hill, Toynbee, and all their unnumbered following, have surely been among the greatest of the pioneers of the Kingdom. As society attains to new convictions about practical issues it will always insist on expressing them through the statute book as well as in other ways.

But for all that, this question of method remains a central one for all who love the Kingdom. The Kingdom cannot be built unless the spirit of the Kingdom is living in human hearts. A hundred well meant Acts of Parliament which are dead letters constitute a warning to us that measures which are merely engineered into being by propagandist methods, and which do not express national convictions, are wholly vain. The mere political boss, the hustling propagandist, the big financier, and the commander of big battalions, are not among the people Christ needs. His work cannot be done in their ways. It is the meek, the poor in spirit, the sufferers, and the lovers whom He needs for His divine ends. They alone create the conditions out of which the Kingdom can arise. In a word, what does build the Kingdom of Heaven is love. The very essence of the faith of Jesus about human affairs was that "love never faileth." It is stronger than money, more effective than armies, more triumphant than bribes and corruption, more enduring than even self-interest. The servants of the Kingdom are, indeed, called to overcome the world, but they are to do it by sympathy, by kindness, by persuasion, by sacrifice, by suffering—if need be by death. All the arts of love are needed. If they were to overcome by force or political cunning, it would prove at once that their victory was worthless for the ends of the Kingdom. One greathearted lover is of more use to Christ than a score of past masters in the art of political manipulation. Constantly it must seem that the way of progress for the Kingdom is blocked by old abuses which can only be shattered by political action, and often the necessary political changes delay their coming almost interminably and intolerably. But people who can love can always get on with the work of the Kingdom. It is growing a little every day by the work of every soul that hopes unconquerably, believes unswervingly, and loves without counting the cost.

Of course, it is hard to bend one's self to this method. Hot blood, eager and generous passion, righteous indignation, bitterness, and hatred that takes to itself the garb of righteousness, must all come under control before any of us can be of much use to Christ, or bring the day of the Kingdom any nearer.

No one who knew ever said it was easy to follow Christ.

All this may well lead us to a further point

with which I may end this chapter. Persistently and earnestly Jesus used to warn His disciples that following Him would lead to trouble with other men. "Beware of men: for they will deliver you up to the councils, and will scourge you in their synagogues. . . . Ye shall be hated of all men for my name's sake. . . . If they have called the master of the house Beelzebub, how much more shall they call them of his household."

We are apt to think that these prophecies related only to the days of the early Church, and have no relevance for us. It is generally assumed that the days of persecution are over and that a follower of Christ may now expect to be allowed to live a quiet life without interference. But if we began to live simply and honestly on the principles of the Kingdom we should probably very soon find out that the days of persecution are *not* over. Persecution does, of course, take very different forms from age to age. Bodily persecution would not now be tolerated by the common conscience of mankind. So far, at least, mankind as a whole has moved. Further, history has shown that physical persecution is a singularly unsuccessful method of combating Christianity. The blood of the martyrs has always proved the seed of the Church. Persecution is now much more cunningly adapted to its intended victims. Ordinary church members are not generally reckoned today to be very heroic Christians, but if the choice betwen an explicit denial of Christ and immediate death were offered to them, I believe that the vast majority would promptly choose death.

It is by much more subtle methods that most of us are led into disloyalty. The people who begin to break with the common conventions of society which involve uncounted compromises with the principles of the Kingdom are immediately looked on with surprise and dislike. At their best they are upsetting persons, and are therefore a nuisance. At the next stage they find themselves being called cranks, or fanatics. Other men and women are not comfortable with them and quietly exclude them from their society. They begin to find themselves lonely. Some are lonely in their own homes—some in their former social circles—some in business circles, where to be excluded from the common fellowship may mean serious money loss. Such people are at once held to be unsuitable for the higher posts in the professions, and though that should not trouble the wholly surrendered disciple, it does trouble most of us who are at best on the way to thorough discipleship. Some men after committing themselves to what seemed to them the Christian way, have seen the woman they loved looking at them with cold amazement and utter misunderstanding. And that is for many a harder thing to face than the stake. Some have found their friends slipping away from them one by one. Some have turned their employers into enemies just by the same method. In special cases it will happen every now and then that the Press will take up the cry and hound with scornful epithets the man who is trying to be loyal. Even the Christian institutions can hardly help adding to the trials of such a man. They have sanctioned certain conventional ways. In our time they have so far made terms with mammon, that thousands who are living for money yet find themselves not intolerably uncomfortable within their borders. Many of them have accepted as insurmountable the ordinary class distinctions. And the would-be-out-and-out member of the Kingdom wounds the susceptibilities of such institutions. He challenges their compromises. He is an innovator, and inevitably is held to be arrogant and impertinent. He disturbs that false peace which most of us have learnt to love. And thus those who in our day may dare to attempt a thorough discipleship are almost sure to find that their path is a lonely one, even within the Christian societies.

These inevitable experiences have all the power of definite persecution to deter the timid follower. But if such men turn to Christ with complaints that His way is very hard, they will have a strange experience. He will say to them in effect, "What did you expect? The disciple is not above his Master. If men hated Me, it is to be expected that they will hate you. No man can come after Me who will not take up some cross daily. Is your cross as heavy as Mine?"

I am constantly being afresh amazed at the number of people who expect that their religion should make them comfortable, and should merely soothe them. Men coming away from church where their consciences have been pricked, or where they have been compelled to suspect that their religion is not

quite the genuine Christian article, complain that
they went for comfort, and have been upset; that
their spirits were longing for refreshment, and that
instead they have had their views outraged. But
Christ only promised rest to those who had taken
His yoke upon them, and Christian rest is only such
as is consistent with the wearing of a yoke. The
disciple's soul may indeed dwell on the heights
where the breezes of the divine joy blow for the
renewing of life. But in the disciple's daily life
there is sure to be a cross if he is following his
Master. He has to be a man at war with the world.
If he makes peace with the world he has denied
Christ.

About that we should do well to be clear before
we begin to attempt to follow. "I have come," He
said, "to set a man at variance against his father,
and the daughter against her mother, and the
daughter-in-law against her mother-in-law. And a
man's foes shall be they of his own household." It
may very well be so—exactly so—with some today
who resolve to follow the real Jesus. And it is sure
to be the case that with pangs of heart a man finds
himself constrained to part company with some
whom he has dearly loved. To face enemies is
almost an easy thing. But to see the backs of one's
friends is a far harder thing. Let no man imagine
he is safe even from that, if he means to follow
Christ.

CHAPTER V

WAS THAT ALL?—THE KING

So far I have spoken mainly of the demand which Jesus makes of men, and of the programme for life which He offers them. Give yourselves up entirely, He said, and then live for the Kingdom—for the reign of Brotherhood. And that, no doubt, *is* the way to life. Those who have tried it are eager to assure us of the complete success of that method. It does bring life to the individual, and it does bring salvation to society. Beyond question, too, there is something splendid in the whole programme thus proposed. It is very difficult, but only the more splendid on that account. It is impossible not to feel that heroism touched its highest point in Jesus, and that there is something essentially heroic even in the attempt to follow Him.

There must, however, be a great many people to-day who will want to say, "But all that does not meet my case at all." Such people are not exactly worrying about their sins in the conventional sense. They are often quite eager to maintain that things which the Church has called sins are not sins at all, but rather advisable forms of experience. But for all that, they are out of harmony with life. They are perplexed, but with a perplexity which they themselves can hardly describe. Something is wrong somewhere, and it is something fundamental. They do not know exactly what they want, but it is certainly something they have not got.

Many of them have no wish to deny the faith of their fathers, but they are discovering that they themselves have no special faith. In particular the war has for hundreds of thousands destroyed all possibility of falling back on any easy-going faith. The obvious facts of the world today are blatantly against all rosy views. Optimistic cries like, "God's in His heaven, all's right with the world," are an intolerable mockery to men who have seen the salient, or the ravaged areas, or who have sat through bombing raids among civilians. Such things have for many a man broken up his old half-conscious beliefs without giving him any new ones; and meantime he is rather sick. He finds most things unsatisfactory—other people, and work, and, after a while, pleasure, and even love—they all pall. At times such men see clearly enough to know that the real fault is in themselves—that it is they who are diseased rather than life itself. They are out of touch all round—with their fathers, and their little brothers, and current politics, and the Church, and the Press. In a word, they have found no reconciliation with their present existence.

And I am very sure that many a man of that kind would say, "All this talk about the Kingdom rather wearies me. I am not in the mood to consider all these vast things which have got to be done; something has got to be done *to me* before I am going to be of any use, or have any satisfaction at all. If all that Jesus had to offer was a vast programme, however magnificent, He does not meet my case." Now what a man in that state is really in need of is some clear conviction about the world he lives in, and the God who rules it. He may not know it, but it is the lack of any such conviction, satisfactory to the mind and congenial to the heart, which is the root of his disease. A man must be able to feel himself at home in this life, if he is ever to know any settled inward peace.

If this world is merely the disordered garden of an incompetent bungler, then no decent man can be satisfied to live in it. If it is the creation of a hostile and mischievous spirit, who takes delight in man's petty flounderings, then the dignified thing would be to go out of the world forthwith. If there is no mind and no heart behind appearances— if we are the sorry victims of mere drift, then indeed anger and humiliation would be justified, and hard to escape from.

Few of us claim to be philosophers, or know what the word means. But for all that *all* of us really, once we have been up against it, want to know something about God. When Tommy at the front said to his chaplain, "Padre, I wish you would tell us what God is like," he was voicing the real need of the hundreds of thousands who are in the state of mind I have tried to describe.

Now this question of what God is like, is the one with which Jesus was most deeply concerned from first to last. It was the central purpose of His life to answer it. All that He said about the Kingdom was really involved in His answer. He was not concerned in the first place to offer men a programme, but a faith. He knew that a programme without a faith is a folly. In this case the programme and the faith are inextricably involved with each other.

Let us look, then, at the way in which Jesus answered the question about God. He did not deal in arguments to prove the existence of God, nor in discussions of any sort about Him. He did not proceed by interpreting His predecessors, or by reasonings from first principles. He was a prophet, not a lawyer or a scholar.

No! what He had done was, firstly, to come to know the Father for Himself. Into that wonderful process of learning and growing intimacy, which must have occupied the first thirty years of His life, we have not been allowed to see; but we do see the result. The result was that He was able to *show* men the Father. He possessed something which He could pass on. He had a clear and radiant vision which He could share with other people, and He lived to pass on to others what He knew.

He did it in various ways. Partly He did it by scattered and spontaneous utterances about God such as, "He clothes the grass of the field," "He sendeth His rain on the just and on the unjust," "He is kind unto the unthankful and the evil." Those who heard Him speak after that fashion must have come to realize that Jesus felt the presence and the handiwork of God in all the beauty and the bounty of nature, and all the ordinary processes of the natural world. Some at least must by association with Him have come to possess that seeing eye which catches some glimpse of God every day even in this troubled world. There were men who even at the front got such glimpses daily—through the songs of the birds whom even the guns could not silence—through the poppies that would grow even among blood-stained trenches—through the sough of cooling winds—through the calm splendour of the stars—and through hundreds of homely deeds of kindness which were inspired by the godlike goodness of ordinary men. Jesus evidently constantly had such glimpses, and those who lived with Him must have learnt to have them too, till they also came to know the Father.

But more particularly He did His work of revealing the Father through definite pictures of Him. With the inspired touch of the world's supreme Master in the use of words, He painted God for us. He did not use abstract words, He preferred to tell the simplest of stories. Two in particular must always stand out. They are both in the fifteenth chapter of Luke. God, He said, is like a shepherd, who though he has ninety-nine of his hundred sheep safe in the fold, must needs go out in the mirk of the night to seek in the desert for the odd and silly one that had got lost. And God is like a father with two unsatisfactory sons—one a silly wastrel, and the other a self-righteous prig—who none the less spends himself in affectionate and endearing services to win them both home, and to share his best with them. Human thought has only soared on that one occasion to that height in expressing God, and there for all time the most sublime conception of Him remains enshrined: A conception surely so sublime as to be the proof of its own truth.

And yet great as these methods proved for Christ's purpose, His supreme method was just to be Himself. He, alone of all men, dared to say, "If you have seen Me you know what God is like." "If you despise Me," He said, "you despise God." "If you receive Me, you receive God." "No man can know God unless he knows what I can show him" (*cp*. John xiv. 9, Luke x. 16, ix. 14, x. 22).

He was, in fact, a God-filled person, and to be with Him was to be learning the truth about God. We get to know God, therefore, by marking all the outstanding things in the life and manner of Jesus. Disease had to give way before Him. Moral poverty exposed itself in His presence to be met by words of hope and good cheer. Little children knew by instinct that here was one with whom they could let go their shyness and be at home. The failures of the world gathered round Him to breathe in a new faith for themselves in the future. Crowds of rough people purposing some corporate evil had again and again to give way before Him. And as we note these things we are progressing in the understanding of God. All the wonderful things which were indicated in the first chapter of this book are facts about God Himself.

The whole three years of the recorded life of Jesus were one long telling of the truth about God for which elsewhere we search so largely in vain. In Jesus it is made so plain that even a child cannot miss it.

Now for the moment let us assume that in all this claim He made Jesus was justified, and that all He showed of God is the very truth. What does it all amount to in relation to the common perplexities of man?

It means, firstly, that this world is a world with love behind it—a world into which a God of love is constantly trying to break. He offers Himself to individuals as a power that can redeem their lives. To broken, tired, and disillusioned men He offers first of all that the past may be blotted out—that the stains on their natures may be cleansed away. He offers to break the chains which bind us to the evil precedents which we have set up for ourselves. In a word, He offers forgiveness. And then He offers power for the future. That good life after which in his heart every man longs becomes a possibility, if what Jesus shows of God is true. Though we are weak in will and inconstant in purpose, a true life is made possible to us because God Himself will dwell within us and live out through us a life after the pattern of Christ's.

It means, secondly, that this world is in the care of One who purposes the Kingdom. Those who labour at it and for it are not disquieting themselves in vain to bend the world into a shape it will not take. They are working in line with the Creator. "Fear not," said Jesus, "it is your Father's good pleasure to give you the Kingdom." Thousands of people feel that the Kingdom is a beautiful conception, but are chilled habitually by a sense that it is too good ever to come true. Nature and human nature are, they believe, against it. Certain evils like war and prostitution always have been and always will be. Servants of the Kingdom are, therefore, no doubt well-meaning idealists, but are up against something permanent in the nature of things which is bound to prove too strong for them. But Jesus never paid any such compliment to evil. The Father of love was on the side of the Kingdom and therefore its coming was in time inevitable. God was not going to be beaten in His own world. He had a confidence about that which the whole confederation of the world's evil powers could not shake, and He invites us to share that confidence.

It means, thirdly, that God means intensely well by every individual on the earth. A hard thing to believe indeed! Of what value to God can all the individuals be among the teeming millions of Europe, Asia, Africa—primitive, rude, and futile creatures? How can even God attach any value to the units in that uncounted stream of petty creatures who have poured across the face of the world all down the ages, buzzing like flies about their petty affairs and then going out into the night? How can even God do more than watch the whole thing with a sort of wholesale benevolence? How dare any one out of the mass suppose that he is noticed from above? Our imagination staggers here. We teach children to say, "God loves me." But for a grown man it is one of the hardest things to say with conviction. How *can* God love individuals? But Jesus, at least, was quite clear about it. "Not a sparrow can fall to the ground without your Father, and ye are of more value than many sparrows. The very hairs of your heads are all numbered." And if we can make a great effort and believe it on the word of Jesus, then indeed life becomes a new thing. We live it before the face of One whose interest in us and love for us are beyond all measure. The universe may *seem* a cold and indifferent affair, but, as a matter of fact, in and through it all a Father is drawing near to us, and watching us with personal and undying affection. Truly, if that is really so a man has nothing to whine about.

But fourthly, if God is really like Christ, then He is a most human God, interested in the most homely affairs. Jesus liked to watch children at their games, and I doubt not knew the rules of them. He was keenly concerned about the ordinary jobs of ordinary men and spoke about them out of intimate knowledge. He was immensely interested in marriage, and spoke of its mystic joys with a beautiful emphasis. He loved society and social occasions, and could always rejoice with those who were happy. And if God is like that, then He is a God a man could love. Most of us in our secret hearts grew up disliking God. What had been told us about Him did little but beget first fear and then repugnance, which we believed to be very wicked, but which was there none the less. But if God is really like Jesus, then it would indeed be a great and splendid thing to be able to have anything to do with Him.

And lastly, if God is like Christ, then God is one who in face of *all* evils bids us hope. He does not hurry things on, it is true. He will not compel men. He lets them sin and live as fools if they will. Evidently He does not want mechanical puppets who go the right way because they are wound up to do it. He wants free men, who have come at last to true life by free choice, even though it be also after many a mistake and bungle. But through it all He loves and hopes and believes in man : loves unto death, believes as only love can, hopes with unconquerable divine persistence.

Now if that is all true, then the secret men are in search of is revealed. If that is all true, then life at once becomes a satisfying and glorious affair. What is really wrong with the perplexed and worried spirits is just that they are lonely. They are lonely with a loneliness which only God could satisfy. And if Jesus was right, then God is waiting to satisfy it at once.

Ah, but is it true? It is clear that Jesus believed all that about God, and embodied it in His own life. It is clear He staked His all on it, and died to manifest it. It is clear, too, that the conviction of its truth persists, and has redeemed this life for thousands. They have found strength and joy and a certain unshakeable peace through believing. Plainly even if it is a delusion it is a most beneficent one.

But is it true? I have admitted that Jesus did

not prove it in any of the ordinary ways which the logical instinct of man expects. Perhaps it only needs a little reflection for any one to see that a fundamental matter like this could not be proved by mere logic, or any of the ordinary scientific inductive methods. But, if so, how can a man be sure about it? How escape from the suggestion that it is only a beautiful dream—the most sublime and exciting of all possible dreams, but still and only a dream?

Now at this point I conceive a man must needs become autobiographical who wants to deal honourably with his fellow-men. If anybody has found a way of becoming certain over this point, he must needs tell others about it or commit the supreme selfishness. And yet all that I have to say is so essentially commonplace that I may well use the plural in saying it. Thousands of people are willing and able to say it too. And what we have to say is really this. We do believe this with a certainty that has become a vital part of us, but we did not come to believe it by way of abstract reasoning. We may hold that a very strong case for this view of God can be made out by pure thinking. We may see, as, for instance, the scientist Romanes came to see so clearly, that reason is at least not against this view. But it was not by a process of reasoning that belief came to us. In a word, Jesus has made us believe it.

We have been in His company a good deal, and when we are there we find we cannot doubt it. By this time it has come to possess us. It has established itself in our most intimate experience and is now part of us. His utter conviction about it has proved irresistible. It was a passion with Him, and that passion is infectious. It has claimed and held us. With many of us, conviction has come bit by bit, but year after year its hold on us has increased. It seems to us that every part of us has become involved in assimilating this faith. Our hearts have leapt up in response to it, and our love has insisted on grasping this truth and holding it fast. Our sense of beauty has been wholly satisfied by it, so that we are moved by this conception to the same sort of emotion as the greatest works of art, or nature at her best, produce. Our wills have been constrained by it, and every act we perform at its bidding makes our conviction the clearer. And if the logical faculty in us has not played much part in this matter, at least our minds have been gripped and filled by the splendour and sublimity of this whole view of the universe. And so, as we have lived with Jesus, it has come to pass that with every power in our beings we absorb His faith, till at times it seems that our whole natures are living in vital response to His mind.

Even though it were shown to us that no absolutely "doubt proof" demonstration of this truth can be offered to men, yet none the less we are willing to stake our all on its being true. If this be the venture of faith we are willing to make it and it does not seem to us much of a venture, when we have Jesus on our side. It seems to us the easiest and the most obvious thing to trust that man.

One rather simple way in which this can be stated is to point out that either this whole view of God and human life is true, or else Jesus was a deluded and dangerous fanatic. But that view of Jesus is simply untenable to those who look at Him honestly. Men call Him an impossible idealist, but only because they have not looked fairly at Him. In some ways He was a very stern realist. He would not shut His eyes to any of the things which have moved others to despair and cynicism. He went through experiences which made Him weep. He drank to the dregs the cup of knowledge—tragic and heartbreaking knowledge. Whatever faith He had it was sustained in full view of all the open facts in one of the darkest hours of the world's life. No! it is impossible to write Him down as a deluded fanatic. And it is equally impossible to write Him down as a deceiver. He said these things so often and so movingly, that if they are not true He was indeed a lifelong deceiver. If He was not the express image of the Father He was the last embodiment of blasphemy. And that is an impossible view of Him. By every hour of His life, and by every feature of His personality, He gives the lie to that suggestion. Of the only two alternatives offered us here one is impossible, and we needs must fall back on the other—namely, the conclusion that Jesus was right.

And yet, while I have thought this point worth putting, I do not think it has been by facing such alternatives that as a matter of fact most of us have come to believe. What I said before is the real truth about that: Jesus has made us believe as He believed. We have come into some sort of moral or spiritual contact with Him, and it has come to pass that we cannot but think as He thought. He is a self-evidencing person. All that is deepest and best in us unites to constrain us to say as we know Him, "Here is of all men the one most certainly to be trusted." It is not simply an emotion with us. Our verdict about Him is a symphony in which all the faculties of our being play a part. To deny Him our implicit trust would now mean violating our whole natures.

And so to any man who is perplexed and out of harmony with life—to any man who feels he needs to find life's secret, and to come somehow to reconciliation with life, and people, and the world in general, I have simply this to say—Concern yourself with this man Jesus. Absorb the truth about Him. Make Him the companion of your mind and heart. And it cannot but be that in time you will discover that He has given you a faith—a faith which redeems the whole of life, and turns it from a puzzled fumbling with distracting mysteries into a glorious, romantic, and magnificent enterprise.

CHAPTER VI

WHAT DOES HE WANT YOU TO DO?

A GREAT many men who feel the attraction of Jesus of Nazareth are none the less intensely repelled by the suggestions which are made to them by those who try to enlist them for the Christian side of life.

1. *The Question of Reserve.*—Anglo-Saxons are naturally reserved people. God seems to have made them that way. No doubt they often overdo their reserve to their own great loss, but it is also an element of great strength. Many of them do not readily or easily show their feelings, and yet by that very fact keep their feelings sincere and strong. And such men often feel that the call to be a Christian is a call to break through their own reserve. They feel they are being summoned to display their feelings and to expose the hidden things of the spirit. Insistent evangelists create the impression that they are trying to break down the natural spiritual chastity of their hearers and to invade the soul's secrets.

And this is why so many men literally hate revivalistic meetings. They shun sentimental excitements because of a deep-seated instinct. If by chance they are carried away by feeling in some public gathering, they are sore and ashamed after-

wards, and take great care to run no further risks
of that sort.

No doubt emotion has a central place in life. It
is the force that runs the world. Mere intellectual
convictions have little power until they become
passionate, and the man who cannot feel deeply will
never accomplish great things. But emotion does
not need to be displayed in corporate ecstasies. It
is meant to produce action, and a man has a large
right to keep his emotions to himself until he can
express them in action. In meetings where men
and women revel in their own emotions, there is
great danger that emotion should become an end in
itself, and when that happens sincerity of character
is at once threatened.

I do not want to criticize those people whose
natural temperament makes it congenial to them to
indulge in corporate displays of emotion, or to suggest for a moment that the spirit of God is not truly
at work in many mass religious movements, but
I do think it quite plain that Jesus made no demand
upon men for the display of emotion. As I search
the gospel pages I find that a strange absence of
excitement characterized the whole movement there
described. Once or twice the crowd seems to have
broken out into exuberant joy, but on the whole
it was a very quiet movement—very quiet, and
simple, and honest, and deep. Jesus never forced
Himself upon anybody. He never invaded the personality of any man. He never asked intrusive
questions, or indulged in aggressive persuasions.
Men came to Him and told Him of their own wills

all the deepest secrets of their lives, and He was always ready to share such secrets and help men out and on. But His characteristic method was to declare His message, and thereafter simply to welcome all who came to Him to offer their loyalty. Plainly there was in His heart a passionate longing after all men. But He would not try to force anybody—not even with emotional forces.

I have heard it again and again complained concerning some Christian Unions in universities that their members have alienated the sympathies of good men and women, and that they have done it by a certain well-meant aggressiveness, and by appearing to ask of students an emotional display of their religion.

I do not think that such Christian Unions can claim to be following any precedent in the life of Christ.

2. *The Matter of Belief.*—A second thing that has repelled many from all organized Christianity is that they have been made to feel that they are being called upon to say they believe what in their hearts they know they do not believe. The duty of faith has often been so presented as to make it seem the duty of achieving a kind of wholesale "swallow," by which all the difficulties of belief are got over once for all. Many a man when presented with Christian doctrine has felt "but believing this would for me be like believing that two and two make five." And to such men it has often been said, "Well, you must just take it on trust, and believe it all the same!" On these terms many a man is

left feeling that he must choose between mental honesty and faith.

But the word faith is really misused when it is handled in this way. When certain truths come home to men in experience so that they become inwardly convinced of them, they may be said to hold them by faith. They hold them, and that with clear certainty, even though they cannot give a full intellectual account of them, or defend them by mere reasoning. They do not believe without proof, but it is personal and experimental proof. "That which we have seen and heard declare we unto you." That is the attitude of people whose belief is a matter of faith. But the word "faith" is misapplied when used in reference to historical statements, or reasoned theological propositions. The criterion of history is criticism, and the criterion of reasoned statements is reason. To ask men to accept either the one or the other by an act of blind submission in which reason is kept in suspense is to offer them an outrage, and to tempt them to dishonesty.

And here again I find in the methods of Jesus no trace whatever of this attitude. He did ask from men a great act of moral submission, but He never tried to force the mind of any one. The disciples found Christianity a very hard thing to *do,* but they did not find it hard to understand. Christ never tried to crush the mind. He was not in the first instance concerned with the matter of intellectual belief at all, and when His religion is presented to men simply as a series of propositions about God and man, life and eternity, it is misrepresented. What Jesus offered to men was primarily a wonderful and largely new conception of God. But He did not argue about this conception, nor embody it in any doctrinal form. It was to Him an immediate apprehension of the soul, and He tried to lead men on till it became that with them, too. It was a view of God which is not contradicted by reason, but which is beyond reason in the sense that reason alone could not attain to it. In life and word Jesus embodied it. He expressed it in immortal pictures. He lived it. And so men gained it from Him. He still wants men to gain it from Him in the same way.

No doubt after He had done His work there was a great deal left to think out. Perhaps there always will be. Because men have acute intellects, they must always want to think out the whole conception of the universe which the Christian view of God implies. And that may take many centuries yet. Because of certain irrepressible instincts within us, we shall probably till the end of time want to sit down before the ultimate mysteries and try with all our mental power to penetrate them. But such activities are not essential to Christian living, and a man is not called upon to hold to any particular solution of the problems of the intellect before he begins to follow Christ. There always have been large numbers of Christians of the Thomas type, for whom the one question that mattered was, "What does He practically want me to *do?*" The place of theology in human life will always be an honoured place. But its place is not in the porch of the house into which men go seeking fellowship with Jesus.

3. *The Fear of Being Unusual.*—A third thing that keeps men and women from any final decision about Christ is the fear that if they submitted themselves to Him He might call upon them to do something unusual, extraordinary, and even unconventional. And how most of us do shudder at the very thought of having to do something "which is not done." Now this suspicion, I believe, is entirely justified. I feel sure that Jesus will call on any man who comes to Him to do very extraordinary and unusual things. He sent seventy of His first followers on a campaign of field preaching which must have made many of them shiver with nervousness beforehand. He has sent stay-at-home souls to the ends of the earth, and timid souls to do such things as street preaching, and so on. If you have not in you a spirit that is willing to take risks and dare strange things, you cannot deal with Christ. He does *not* want you to remain simply a conventional Briton, for notoriously the conventional Briton is not yet Christian.

But it is equally certain that Jesus will send no man to a job beyond his strength, and that He will ask no man to act without conviction. Men who were at the stage of hesitation have often said to me, "But I can't do anything. I couldn't teach kids to save my life. I could never possibly speak or pray in public. I hate meetings of all sorts. I feel sure I could never play up." Well, the answer to such men is, I am sure, that they will never be asked to do things which they cannot do, though it is certain that they will be asked to do things which they don't want to do. They are certain to come to points in the Christian way when they shrink and shiver and would give anything to be allowed to go back. Christ had at one point to go to the cross, and His whole being seems to have risen up in a shrinking revolt. Yet He went. On a lower plane such hours come to all His followers. They, too, want to revolt, but if they are really followers they, too, go. Only, as I said, Jesus does not leave us without the necessary convictions to support us. When you become *quite* sure that to do some unusual thing is for you the right thing—when you see it clearly as a part of your Christian discipleship, then you *can* do it. It is when you are still in doubt that you feel a fool in doing strange things. Many a man ere this has allowed others to cajole him into trying to do some unusual or extreme thing, which in his heart he was exceedingly doubtful about. And such men have indeed felt fools both at the time and afterwards. But no man ever feels a fool when he tries to act on a conviction. The real trouble is that he is apt to find that he is more of a coward than he wishes to believe.

Further, it is quite certain that Jesus never gives the wrong job to the wrong man. If you really cannot "teach kids," then you will not be called upon to do it, though it is the finest work the world offers. If you are no organizer, you will not be asked to organize. If you are no speaker, you will not have to speak, though it is still unfortunately possible that you will not be prevented. What Jesus really wants of every man is the exercise of the gifts which God has given him, not the exercise of gifts which have been withheld. He would have you fulfil yourself—not misuse or distort yourself. The body of Christians in your immediate world may not be as wise as Christ in this matter, and may try to put force upon you. But Jesus puts that kind of force on no man. When you follow Him you may have a dangerous and uncomfortable time, but you will at least have the joy of acting on conviction and of trying to use some gift which you possess.

4. *What He Does Want.*—Can we then say what Jesus does want us to do? I believe we can, and although I have touched on this point in Chapter II., I gladly return to it to examine it more fully.

We can put it to begin with by saying that Jesus wants every man to discover what is for him the call of God, and then to follow. There is a call of God for every man. He made us for His glory, and there is no man or woman among us who cannot live to that glory. The one essential is that we discover our call. It is not always an easy thing to do, but some general things may be said about it. It is certainly not a call to do nothing—to live on your means and amuse yourself, however innocently. It is certainly not a call to the way of least resistance, because most dogmatically Jesus insisted that there is always a cross in it. It is not a call just to swim with the tide. The people of Jesus have always found the world against them.

The way in which Jesus Himself put it was to say that it is a call to "Seek first the Kingdom of Heaven." That means this, that the man or woman who decides to close with Christ must resolve to use the whole of life, and all the talents which he or she may possess, for the purpose of setting up the Kingdom of Heaven. In other words, what is at stake in this matter is the whole business of a man's aim in life. The conventional life purpose is "to get on in life"—to make money—to improve one's position—and then to settle down in comfort. That cannot be reconciled with Christian discipleship, though notoriously it is often reconciled with church membership. Christ's terms are that we seek *first* the Kingdom—that all personal aims be subordinated to that. We are to live to extend the reign of God in every department of life—domestic, social, industrial, commercial, political, and international. And having that aim such things as a man's own prosperity, or fame, or wealth, or ease, must be held quite secondary.

That is the great issue which a man must face who would decide for Christ. And beyond all doubt it is likely to cost most of us many a wrestle in the night, and many a day of agony. I have read that when the call of God came to Shaftesbury—the call to give himself to the cause of the maltreated victims of industry—he saw at once that it would cut at the roots those political ambitions in which he had been brought up, and that he lay upon his bed writhing in grim agony while he tore from his heart his darling desires. He was no exception. To turn one's back upon oneself means a terrific struggle for most of us. And that is the struggle to which Christ summons us—not to sentimentalism, or the swallowing of doubtful dogmas. We are to crucify personal ambition. And it will always be for many so hard a thing that going through the throes of it will mean actual fellowship with the sufferings of Him who endured the cross.

When, however, we have got that point clear I believe our thought is apt to take a fatally wrong turn. Many men who become sure that Christ is calling them to a religious vocation also believe that He is calling them *out* of life's ordinary vocations. They think that they must take up one of those ways of life which are conventionally called religious—that they must become ministers, or missionaries, or agents of religious societies, and so forth. Perhaps we are misled by the fact that the first disciples had to leave their fishing, and become for the rest of their lives itinerant evangelists. But we should not be misled by that fact if we stopped to remember that while Jesus needed those special men for special purposes, He was also calling *all* men unto Him.

Now it may be that there are some ordinary callings which will have to be utterly forsaken by Christian disciples. If a calling cannot be exercised *ad majorem dei gloriam,* it will have to go. I have a pretty clear persuasion to that effect in the case of bartenders and bookmakers, and at least grave suspicions about a few other common callings. But I am sure that the callings which stand condemned by Christ are all of them callings which are socially harmful, and which therefore stand condemned by the interests of society.

But once we have recognized that point, then it is possible to say that Jesus does not want men to change their occupations, but to employ those very occupations as methods of forwarding the Kingdom. All the normal occupations of civilized men are capable of being made into religious vocations. It is not necessarily more Christian to be a parson than to be a first class lawyer, or a commercial man of the finest kind, or a good bootmaker, or a first rate shop hand.

Christian vocation is something so wide and comprehensive that it covers the whole of human life. We tend naturally to exalt some callings above others. I suppose, for instance, that all men at least would agree in putting first among great human vocations that of the real mother. But this grading of occupations is really a mistake. All the occupations which are necessary to the complex life of man are capable of being exercised in such a way as to bring the Kingdom further into being, and for that reason they are all really equally honourable, and religious.

Therefore I conceive that the man who would follow Christ is called upon to choose his occupation as wisely as he can in view of his circumstances and abilities, and then to learn to regard his occupation as *his* way of forwarding that Kingdom. The

Kingdom has not yet been built, partly because a great many good people have thought of it as something to be worked at in their spare time—on Sundays and in the evenings. It can never so be built. It will come into being only as men learn to submit their daily callings to the control of its principles. For my part, and as I see the present situation, it seems plain beyond question that the supreme need of Christ today is not the need of ministers to proclaim the principles of the Kingdom, but the need of grim and resolute practical men who will enter the arena of ordinary life with those principles as their orders, and will grapple with the terrific problem of conforming our actual life to the pattern shown us in the mount. When we have big business men, and big employers, and big labour leaders, and big financiers, and big lawyers, whose one aim in life is to set up the Kingdom of God, and that without considering what is going to happen to them in the by going, then the Kingdom of God will be getting really near. But though I mention a few occupations in this way as examples, the same thing is true of them all. If a man's occupation is necessary to the wholesome life of mankind—if he is not ministering to diseased cravings and unwholesome wants—if he is not a parasite or a trafficker in senseless luxuries, but one who supplies something which true human life requires, then his calling is at once capable of being transformed into an instrument for building the Kingdom, and Christ does not ask him to forsake it, but rather to make it something greater than it has been.

Let me amplify this point by considering the case of Industry a little further. We use the word to cover all those forms of mental, manual, and mechanical dexterity through which the material needs of the world are supplied. It must therefore always be the case that, along with agriculture, industry must always fill the lives of nearly three-quarters of mankind.

Now theoretically considered it is surely plain that there is something truly splendid about industry. It represents a million triumphs of the mind and brain in utilizing nature and bending matter to the service of man. It provides opportunity for the exercise of the creative faculty in man, which is among his very highest faculties. It might provide endless opportunities for team work, or that cooperation in big undertakings which brings a divinely sweet joy into life. When it results in securing that any body of people are well housed, clothed, fed, and warmed—when it provides them with convenient transit, and eases for them the burden of life—when it produces stately cities, and noble buildings—when in fact it brings it to pass that the friction and labour of ordinary life are reduced to a minimum, then surely it achieves a very noble result. There will certainly be no Kingdom of Heaven on earth until industry is redeemed, and constitutes in itself an illustration of the working of the principles of the Kingdom. Yet what is it today? A notoriously unhappy and unstable thing. To millions the conditions that maintain within the industrial world seem to shut out God.

They are not conscious that they are fulfilling themselves in any noble or useful way within its borders, but are in a state of constant revolt against its principles. Because there is a constant state of warfare within that world the whole of human life is soured for millions. Employers often feel this acutely, and wage earners feel it still more so. Men have often smiled at me as if I were some strange kind of fool, when I have suggested that a man should exercise his Christianity within his working hours. "Why," they have said, "life in a workshop is one long and bitter fight, and how can that possibly be made a religious occupation?" A great many business men are quite blunt about the matter. "Christianity," they say, "simply cannot be applied to business. Business is a matter of struggling for your own hand, and the man who would survive in the business world must be smart and alert, and vigilant for number one."

What lies below all these sayings is, of course, the fact that industry and commerce are wrongly based morally. "The foundations of society are wrong, because the relations between man and man are wrong. Jesus told us to love one another, but as a plain matter of fact we do not love one another."[1] That is what makes industry and commerce such bitter things, and destroys the spiritual life of so many who are involved in their struggles.

And so plainly there is going to be no Kingdom of God in the world until industry and commerce are radically transformed—until the motive of

[1] *The Call to Battle*, Student Christian Movement.

service takes the place of desire for private gain as the mainspring of them both—until all harsh rivalries are removed from their workings. That transformation presents itself to my mind as the greatest task which was ever proposed by the will of God to the wills of His children. It is going to call for all that is greatest in man—for the exercise of his intelligence, his ingenuity, his organizing ability, his moral powers of self-restraint and unselfishness, his imagination, and his heart. But unless and until it is done this can never be a Christian country. So long as three-quarters of our people are for eight hours a day subjected to the influence of a great system which is not Christian, so long will it be absurd to expect to see them growing in Christian character. For the evangelization of Britain in the true sense of the word the transformation of industry is essential.

And now let us come back to this question of what Jesus wants a man to do. For the great majority of men life is going to be lived within the industrial and commercial world. Is it not plain that Jesus must want a great army of men and women within that world who will set themselves to help in the gigantic task of this vital and tremendous transformation? A comparatively small proportion of us may be wanted in such callings as the ministry. But the great mass of us are wanted for this central and more difficult calling.

I believe this is the form in which the challenge of Christ is coming to the young of this generation. Some solution of the problem of industrial unrest must be found or we are undone. And there can be no abiding solution but Christ's solution. Will the young, and able, and virile of this present hour dare to accept Christ's leadership and in His name go to this battle? It will be necessary, of course, not only to have manual workers and captains of industry working at the matter. Lawyers will be needed to help in working out the new organization and in giving it legal form. Teachers will be needed who will help to train the kind of men and women who can work a Christian system. Writers, artists, and journalists will be needed to embody the ideals of the Kingdom in such shapes of beauty as will capture the imagination and satisfy the soul. The Kingdom will never come fully till we all help, and meantime it is certain that there is a place in its working ranks for any man or woman with any power of any sort.

Some who read these words may mean to be doctors, and for them what all this means is just— By all means be doctors, but be sure you are doctors who live not for fees but for health, not for your advancement but for the common good. Some may mean to go into business, and to them what this message comes to is—Certainly go into business, but go with the purpose of transforming business into something which will be conducted on the principles of the Kingdom, and reckon *now* with the fact that if you go with that purpose you will probably never be rich, and may indeed be very poor. "Though He was rich yet for our sakes He became poor." Some may mean to take up teaching either in school or university, and the word to them seems to be—What better could you do, but see to it that you do not become a mere place hunter, who merely does his work because it is necessary to do it in order to draw a salary, but a man or woman who lives to teach truth, and in that and other ways to serve the younger lives you touch. Some may mean to take to agriculture or forestry or mining or scientific research, or the civil services, etc., etc.; and to all such the same things may be said. One and all, these callings are capable of being made notable forms of service for the Kingdom of God. When they are so regarded they become worthy of all that is greatest in man. When they are otherwise looked at they are mere divergent ways of petty self-seeking.

No doubt it will take a good deal of thinking on the part of individuals to find out just exactly how their particular duties and opportunities may be used for the sake of the Kingdom. There is much real discovery to be achieved still in this direction. And Christ's disciples will have to get together, that they may think and work together over such concrete questions. I believe that when the Church rises to the actual calls of our day it will offer to the men of any particular trade or profession opportunities for thinking out together how that particular trade or profession may be so transformed as to make its pursuit a method of realizing the Kingdom. And I fancy that such discussions of intensely practical issues are likely to prove both more interesting and more profitable than the discussions of theo-

retical questions which once so heated the nominal
followers of Jesus. Possibly, too, the ministers of
the future are going to find that people have very
little use for mere listening, and when the sermon
has been at least partially dethroned to make way
for cooperative study of the will of Jesus, the
coming of the Kingdom may be greatly hastened.

One last thing must be said before this chapter
closes. It is simply this—that all those who in the
sense here indicated are going to accept the call of
Christ, are so surely as the sun rises going to find
themselves "up against it." The man who tries to
do business on Christian lines will not only lose
money by it at first, but he is sure to be called a
fool. He will find his trade or his business associ-
ates getting angry with him. If he is in an employers' association he may have a very bad time
of it. If he is a Trade Unionist he may have some
very heavy risks to face. If he is an employee he
will very often make his employer angry. He will
probably find himself passed over when promotions
are going. Indeed, he will often get the sack, and
find himself facing a hostile world not knowing
what is to come next. The world will not want
such men, and it will probably try to starve them
out. To set out on the path of discipleship may
seem at first a great and inspiring adventure, but
afterwards tribulation and persecution are sure to
arise, and it will then be seen whether by such things
the would-be disciple is going to be offended.

Yes, Christian discipleship is as hard as all that!
It would be well to reckon with the fact to begin

with. Among the things He wants you to do this is certainly one. He wants you to be willing to face the scorn and opposition of men for His sake and the Kingdom's. And the scorn and opposition may at times be very bitter and drastic.

Is it worth it? Does He deserve such things from His followers? If you are not *quite* sure that the answer to these questions is *Yes* then you are not yet ready to set out with Him.

CHAPTER VII

WHAT ABOUT HUMAN NATURE?

OF those who reach this point in this volume, a number must, I am sure, have wanted ere this to break in with the exclamation, "This is all very beautiful and fine, but it is also hopelessly idealistic. These suggestions as to a way of life are far too high and hard for ordinary people. In fact, the whole programme is simply not practicable in view of what human nature is." I notice that many people are made impatient to the point of anger by having such suggestions put before them, and that they are apt to demand a religion that does not ask so much, and is therefore more suited to what they call average humanity. Such people are often heard insisting that "human nature is human nature"—that "selfishness will out"—that the mean and cowardly elements in mankind are ineradicable and must therefore be reckoned with, and that the well-meaning enthusiasts who call us all to sublime ways of life are really wasting their time. Men have said to me repeatedly, "Oh, at times I feel inclined to attempt that way of life, but at other times I find I can't rise to it, and want something easier. I am sure, therefore, that I could not keep it up, and it seems to me that the honest thing to do is to make no pretence of being Christian."

Beyond all question the world's attitude to Jesus is that He was a well-meaning idealist, but that He is also hopelessly impracticable as a leader for ordinary life. The idea of taking Him seriously either in international or home politics, in business or in industry, has not yet been honestly entertained by any nation. This is still the real attitude even of thousands who attend church. If it were reported that a Chamber of Commerce or a House of Commons had paused in its proceedings that the members might quietly consider, "What is the mind of Christ about this business which we have in hand?" the news would electrify the world. It is not only Germans who think that *"real politik"* is something too serious and hard to be brought into honest relation to the thought of Jesus.

Now whether it be right or wrong it is certain that this common attitude is the most powerful of all the obstacles to progress in the Christian sense. Men declare things to be impossible, and so long as that conviction holds the field they *are* impossible. So long as men are in that state of mind they cannot honestly try to realize Christ's purposes. We must believe that things are possible before they can become possible. All who have ever worked for the cause of Purity must have found that the supreme difficulty they have to face is just callous scepticism about any real change. It is that scepticism which leads men to declare concerning such evils as prostitution, "Oh, these things have always been and they always will be," or in other words, "Human lust will always prove too strong for moral reformers." The same thing appears in connection with war. By far the most dangerous force in society today in that connection is the widespread opinion that man is incurably a fighting animal, and that therefore no league of nations or other covenants of peace can ever be really effective. Thus, though men long for peace and know something of the degradation of war, they succumb beforehand to the menace of a brute instinct.

Exactly the same thing appears in connection with the controversy over competitive commerce and industry. A great many people assume it as axiomatic that the only effective spur to effort for the great majority of mankind is the hope of private gain, and that to trust to any other motive whatever would result in letting the wheels of efficient effort run down.

To this extent a low view of man holds the field, and disinclines men and women from taking Jesus seriously.

And it must be admitted in view of this whole contention that there is something in it. The "something" that is in it produced those sepia stained pages in which Calvinists have written of the total depravity of man, and his entire inability in his natural state to do any good thing.

To understand Calvin it is only necessary to watch the crowd of men and women in any large city at their weekly Saturday revels, or to find out the real facts in connection with any great social evil, such as cheating in business, or drink, or impurity. We would all like to hold wholeheartedly the most optimistic views about mankind, but the facts which have emerged in the last year or two alone, about profiteering, about sexual laxity, and about intemperance, are enough in themselves to chill all easy optimism. Rather are we all constrained to say, "There is no hope of any Kingdom of Heaven on earth—indeed, there is no hope of a just state of society unless these men can be changed." Or in other and older words, "There is no hope for the world unless there can be found a 'remedy for sin.'" It is good to get things down to simple words. The real issue here is whether or no we believe that sin can be overcome. If it can, then ideals are not impracticable things. If it cannot, then it is waste of time even to talk about them.

What of Jesus then? It is certain to begin with, as I have repeatedly said, that His idealism was not based upon any ignorance of the real evils of life, or the deep-seated evil in man. He knew all that Calvin knew—all that modern sceptics in connection with morals know. But He also saw other things in man, because of which He believed that men and women will respond to the love of God once it is fairly revealed to them. He saw in man something which made it seem worth while to die for man. He believed, as thousands have come of late to believe, in the wonderful latent goodness of the ordinary wayward man or woman. He believed that there is in each human being a greater

self than meets the eye, and that that greater self
can be called into life. He believed in fact, if we
like so to put it, that man *can* be saved, and that
He knew the secret of his salvation.

That secret lay in the fact, which was so clear
to Jesus, that God is always at hand to enable the
man who will turn to Him to do things which are
impossible to mere human nature. On one occasion
His disciples discussed with Him the possibility of
a rich man's being saved, and when they had
listened with amazement to Jesus as He declared it
was easier for a camel to go through the eye of a
needle than for a rich man to enter the Kingdom,
they asked with a certain wonder which we can
well understand, "Who then can be saved?" And
to that Jesus made answer, "With men this is impossible, but with God all things are possible." It
was His conviction that if men would but once
get into living relation with God they would become
able to do such things as He did Himself—and even
greater things. He did not propose the Kingdom to
"mere" men, but to men in whom the Father is
willing to live. In fact, His promise, "Ye shall
receive power" is as fundamental a part of His
message as the other words, "Seek ye first the Kingdom of Heaven."

What this means is that our study of the Kingdom message of Jesus is incomplete and really
worthless unless we understand also what is called
His promise of grace. If we go back to the historical Jesus for a programme, and stop there, we
shall do nothing. If that programme is ever to

become a reality we have to learn to live by the present power of God, who is known to us in Christ. What is really meant by grace is just the influence of the living God. And Jesus knew for Himself that that influence is always available, and that through it a man may do and dare the impossible. From moment to moment He lived by it. The great secret He wanted to share with His disciples, and still wants to share with us, is that any man may live by it from moment to moment.

What we are really faced with here is the question of the secret of achievement in human affairs. We are apt to suppose that when men achieve notable results of any sort the explanation lies in the unusual powers which they possess. We look back upon history and say of its outstanding figures that they were men of genius—men with abnormally great brain power, or will power, or with a special endowment of energy. And plainly so long as we rest in that explanation of their lives, we also feel that their lives have very little significance for us. For most of us know with painful certainty that we have no abnormal gifts.

But the great men both of the Hebrew tradition and of the Christian tradition give a quite different explanation of their achievements. Unanimously and whole-heartedly they repudiate the suggestion that there was any special power or genius in them. What they do say is that the constraint of God came upon them and carried them through. All that they had done was not to resist. They were weak things whom God had used—that was the whole story.

The point is so vital that it is worth while to recall some especial instances. Take the case of Gideon to begin with. When he first appears in history it is as a shy discontented man living in an out of the way corner, and wondering why some one did not do something to deliver his enslaved nation. And then the call of God came to him. He could not at first believe it *was* the call of God. He accounted himself one of the least and weakest of the nation. He argued and tried to escape. But God said to him, "Go! have not I sent thee!" and the result was that he saved Israel. Or turn to Jeremiah's story. He was of all the Hebrew heroes the most sensitive, shy, and retiring. His ideal for himself would have been a little country cottage, where with wife and child he might have lived out his days undistracted by public affairs. But the constraint of God came upon him. It was, he says, like a smouldering fire shut up in his bones, and, though he, too, held back for long, the day came when he was weary with forbearing and could not stay. He had to go, and going he played one of the most heroic and effective parts ever played by any man of his nation.

The same story is told by the Psalmists, one after another. "I will not trust in my bow, neither shall my sword save me, but Thou hast saved us." "The mighty man is *not* delivered by much strength." "My soul wait thou only upon God, from him cometh thy salvation." That refrain recurs in Psalm after Psalm. The prophet Zechariah re-echoes the same message: "Not by might nor by power, but my spirit." So does John the Baptist: "A man can take unto himself nothing except it be given him from Heaven." As for St. Paul, it may truly be said to be his characteristic message—the eternal thing in his witness—that God can take the weak things of the world to confound the mighty. Of himself he dared to say, "I can do all things through Christ who strengtheneth me." For all the urgent needs of a difficult and dangerous life he had found that "His grace is sufficient."

And to these testimonies, yet another and a more impressive one must be added. The account which Jesus gave of his own achievements is in the familiar words, "I am not come of myself." "I can of my own self do nothing." "I have not spoken of myself." "The Father that dwelleth in me, he doeth the works." He was not in this essential respect different from his brethren. He, too, lived by a power that came to Him from His Father.

Here, then, is the great secret. The great things of the world's history have not been done merely by the power of human brains and genius—not by resoluteness of will, and enormous exertions of self-directed energy. They have come to pass through men and women who yielded themselves up to God to be used by Him, and very often they themselves were vastly astonished at the things which God brought to pass through them.

It is not necessary, in receiving this truth, to depreciate the value of human brains and energy. They are always gifts of God, and are essential to good work. But the truth seems to be that no amount of brains and energy will enable a man to do work of lasting value unless he is constrained by God, and that, on the other hand, every man has at least enough brains and energy to do some work of lasting value if only he will submit to be guided by God.

It would not have seemed to Jesus a reasonable thing if His disciples had turned to Him, and urged Him to remember that they were only weak and ignorant men, so that it was absurd to look to them for the building of the Kingdom. He would merely have told them that God was waiting to work through them, and that, therefore, all things were possible to them. And it would not seem to Jesus a reasonable thing were we to turn to Him and decline the enterprise of the Kingdom on the ground that we are weak and wayward men. God knows that is pitifully true. But Jesus would say to us also that the power of God may rest upon us, that the spirit of God may dwell within us, and that all things may be possible to us too.

Again, let me say Jesus did not propose the Kingdom enterprise to mere men. He proposed it to men in whom God was willing to dwell—to men who might draw from God all needed power even for the gigantic task of that Kingdom. And this is the explanation of the amazing optimism of Jesus. Though men showed their worst to Him, He continued to believe that they would yet respond to His summons, and build the Kingdom. He never paid any evil thing the compliment of believing that it was permanently rooted in the order of things.

He never despaired of humanity. And the reason was that He knew the human heart to be a possible temple for the living God.

All this has a peculiar significance for a very numerous class of men and women in our day. I mean the class of those who quite honestly protest that they are not interested in the matter of personal salvation at all. Sometimes they describe themselves by saying that they don't care about their souls one way or the other. It seems to them a kind of selfishness after all to be bothering about their spiritual condition, and they resent the calls that are still sometimes sounded in their ears bidding them seek security while yet there is time. What such people *are* interested in is the business of making this world a better and a happier place for the mass of men. They do really love others, and in the service of others they are able to forget themselves altogether. Many of them protest that they have no interest in theology, or in most of the talk they hear about religion. What we have got to do, they declare, is to get on with the plain business of loving other people, and there is nothing difficult to understand about that. For that reason they often feel much of the talk that goes on in churches to be simply irrelevant to the real business of life.

I have nothing whatever to criticize in the attitudes here suggested. The man who can and does fill his life with the practical business of loving is, indeed, a kindred soul to Jesus, and if he forgets himself altogether in that preoccupation, he will none the less be living spiritually on the heights. I know of nothing in the gospels which would justify one in asking the man who is successfully obeying the two great commands of Jesus to stop and bother about his soul.

But the trouble with most of us is that we find we cannot successfully obey the two great commands of Jesus. When we set ourselves to serve the world and love all men, we are brought up sharp by the discovery of our own pitiful incompetence. One day temper breaks forth and spoils a whole day's living. Another day indolence lays its paralysing hand upon us, so that some task for the Kingdom goes undone which the night should have seen finished. On a third, some unruly desire escapes from control, and prevents us from living in the Kingdom temper. Or it may be that the weight of our own cares becomes so heavy that we cannot produce unselfish love. Or worldly ambition gets under our guard, and we find ourselves in the ranks of Christ's enemies.

In fact, having set out to reform the world we come to a day when from our heart there bursts the cry, "Who are we to try to reform the world? We need to be reformed ourselves, and until we are we are going to be of no use." It is a critical and horrible hour in a man's life story. While he is in it the beautiful ideals which once inspired him become only mocking memories. In his disillusionment about himself, he is apt to become disillusioned about all other people and about things in general. The danger at that point of turning down the mean by-path which leads to cynicism is very, very great. Because he has tried to redeem the world and has failed miserably, he is apt to assume that the whole suggestion of world redemption is only a foolish dream. Thousands at that point in life have decided to compromise with the world as it is, and have therefore been of no more account for the enterprise of the Kingdom. The ranks of the middle aged are swelled by thousands of men and women who once were idealists, but who have now "settled down." They have not got very satisfied faces. They are not making a specially great thing of life. But they are prepared to argue that it is only foolish to expect more of life than they are finding in it, and that to dream dreams of a new heaven and a new earth as they once did is only a youthful folly, which it is best to outgrow as soon as possible. It is thus that Christ has lost armies of men and women who once appeared to be promising recruits.

But there is another way out of that bad hour in life when a man first discovers his own incompetence. It is the way taken by those who in their need discover the grace of God. Such men find that just because they want to help others they *must* think of themselves. They need not think selfishly, but they must take honest account of their own weakness and inconstancy. Because they would fain help to save the world they *must* first be saved themselves. Salvation truly conceived does not mean being rendered complacently certain that an eternity of bliss awaits us, but being made fit for real service in the Kingdom of God now. Indeed, no man *is* saved until he has forgotten to think about bliss for himself and has learnt to think first of the Kingdom. And if a man who in that sense wants to be saved, turns to Jesus, then Jesus meets him with the old, old promise of grace which is yet new every morning. Put in very simple language, what that promise amounts to is, I conceive, just this—That if we will admit our need and turn to God for strength we are sure to get it. If we give up trusting ourselves and learn instead to trust God, He does not fail us. If we lean on Him, the journey becomes possible. If we feed our beings upon His spiritual resources they prove sufficient to meet the case.

It is exactly for this reason that many men and women find they only live successfully when they daily partake of the eucharist. And of all who ever lived successfully in the Christian sense it is true that they had learnt daily to feed their souls upon Him who is offered to us in the eucharist, although they may not have outwardly partaken of that sacrament.

As I see things, we have here reached the heart of the whole matter—the central truth for all who would fain follow Jesus, or who are interested in the Kingdom. When we have learnt to see our careers in the light of the Kingdom—when we have discovered our vocation in relation to it—we still shall not be able to follow them without the daily help of grace. The artist will need it if he is to deal truly with beauty. The business man will need it, if he is to be inspired for the lofty and difficult calling of Christian business. All who deal with men will need it, if they are to treat men continuously as their brothers. The thinker will need it, if he is to think truly. For the grace of God is as wide as human life. It fits the case of every man who is doing any bit in the great workshop of Christian civilization. It is available for husbands and wives, for fathers and mothers, for sons and daughters, for public servants, for doctors and teachers, for lawyers and accountants, for all who create with hand or head. Without it none of these callings can be made divine. With it they all become ways of extending the Kingdom.

And now it is possible to sum up all that has been said in these pages. The world was made for the Kingdom, for it was made by the Father of Jesus who preached the Kingdom. The human race is waiting for that Kingdom, for in it alone lies the remedy for all the evils which today so tragically afflict it. And the Kingdom *can* be built by ordinary men and women, because to them God will without measure give His extraordinary grace. Because of that, there is no evil thing in the world with power in it to stand against them. There is no kingdom with power to stand against Christ's Kingdom.

To every man and woman there is offered the chance of helping, and only by helping can life be made really great. There is no width or wealth of life comparable to that enjoyed by those who are in the harness of the Kingdom, and in fellowship with God. No man may truthfully plead inability. By the grace of God every man can do something that will really help. The only question that remains undecided for each of us is: "Will we take the grace of God and accept the service: or are we going after all to continue to huddle in the mean and sordid house of self?"

CHAPTER VIII

THE RESOURCES OF THE DISCIPLE

AFTER the disciples of Jesus had lived with Him for some time they became aware that every now and then He was not to be found. He would disappear for a whole night at a time, or would go off into the mountains alone. He would seem to have insisted at all costs on securing such solitude and such quiet.

When they asked Him what He was doing at such times, He told them He was praying. Quite possibly they themselves had never prayed, and had not thought of it as an essential thing in life. Almost certainly they did not know how to pray, and had hitherto been content in spite of the fact. But it cannot have escaped their notice that Jesus came back from His lonely periods of prayer restored both in body and spirit. After very busy and crowded days which had worn out His whole being, He would go away into the quiet and then return to His work with all His great powers of spirit in full and fresh activity. Therefore there came a day when these men who wanted to follow Jesus and work for His Kingdom came to Him and said, "Lord, teach us to pray." They did not know at first how much it would mean to them, but they had at least grasped the fact that one of the secrets of a life of successful service lay in prayer. And that remains a fact.

Perhaps we are hindered at this point by the very word "prayer." To us it possibly suggests the use of certain prayers which we may have learnt, or taking part in some definite form of church service. We shall not understand until we get behind such things. What prayer really means in its essence is recovering a living sense of God's reality and presence. It means some such quiet waiting in spirit as will lead us once again to know that He is with us. When the fretted, weakened, and perplexed man or woman becomes aware that God in unchangeable strength and wisdom and love is at hand, then prayer is achieved. By contact with Him of that sort the spirit of man is restored and quickened. In such hours quietness and courage, hope and energy come back to human beings, and the disciple is made fit for more of the warfare of Christ. The strongest and the weakest here stand together. All alike need to be thus restored again and again if for them the labours of the Kingdom are to be possibilities. We have seen already that the enterprise of the Kingdom is not proposed to ordinary men, but to men filled with the extraordinary grace of God. And what is meant by prayer is really just such an attitude of spirit as shall allow the grace of God to reach the recesses of the nature of man.

No doubt the difficulties of this subject are very real and apparent. They are of two sorts—theoretical and practical. It is difficult to understand how prayer achieves its results, or why it should be necessary, and it is difficult to learn how to pray.

I do not propose to enter on a discussion of the theoretical difficulties of prayer. If we are only to ask what is the will of God it must occur to the simplest minds to wonder why we need to ask God to do what is His will. If He has promised to answer prayer it is difficult to understand why so many eager prayers seem to receive no answer. It is very difficult to think out any intelligible account of how intercession for others achieves great results. Personally I believe that all these difficulties can be fully met. An answer to them is found by experience, and Christian thought has achieved a great deal in the effort to think out the matter. But for a discussion of that whole matter I can only refer my readers to such books as that comprehensive study of the subject, edited by Canon Streeter and called "Concerning Prayer," or to such studies in the teaching of Jesus as Prof. Hogg's "Christ's Message of the Kingdom," or Prof. Fosdick's "The Meaning of Prayer."

What does stand out quite clearly amidst all the mysteries which surround this subject is that by a certain attitude of spirit, which we call the attitude of prayer, men and women do come into some conscious relation to God, and that the constant experience of that relationship is the very secret of all high vitality in a disciple. Only those who practise deliberate silence and quiet are able to hear the still small voice by which God directs His children.

Only those who fall back habitually on His un-
limited strength and unchanging goodness escape
unbearable nervous strains. Few at least are able
habitually to hope in this distracted world unless
they become habitually aware of Him—the quiet,
patient, and all-powerful one. About that the testi-
mony of all the Christian centuries is perfectly clear.
Whether we can understand or not in this connection we can know. I do not happen to understand
how food nourishes the body, being wholly ignorant
of physiology. Nor do I understand how such
waiting on God restores the soul. But I am quite
as sure of the latter as a fact of experience as I
am of the former. Here experience justifies a
really dogmatic statement. Except we learn to
pray we may not hope to achieve much for Christ.

And that brings me to the second difficulty of
this matter—the difficulty not of believing in prayer
but of learning to achieve it. Thousands of people
who have no intellectual difficulties in this connection are almost hopelessly baffled by the practical
ones. Perhaps as children they "said their prayers,"
but when as adults they try to attain to something
more real and vital than that they fail. They declare that they cannot achieve any living experience
of God through prayer. They have tried so often
without success that they have given up the effort,
and are now almost annoyed, and certainly baffled,
by all insistence on the necessity of prayer.

And yet I believe the fact remains that we *must*
learn to pray if we are to be able to serve. Only I
am quite sure that we do not need to learn to pray in

any one way, and perhaps it is just here that many have made a fatal mistake. I use the word "prayer" to cover all the ways in which the human spirit becomes aware of the Divine spirit, and those ways are uncounted.

When Wordsworth during his communion with nature became aware of "a presence which disturbed him with the joy of elevated thoughts," he had attained to prayer at its very highest. Probably a great many are like him, and will only know the best of communion with God when nature, which is His garment, has helped them to realize Him. Plainly many of the Psalmists used nature in this way to rise to a sense of God. The gospels even suggest that Jesus used nature in the same way. And yet to others it has nothing to say. To them the open country is simply dull.

I remember a man who told me in a moment of confidence that he had found God mainly through the sacred experiences which came to him as a husband and a father. Only by knowing something of the sacredness of human love had he been made able to realize the Divine love, and I fancy that to that man his home will always be more of a temple than his church.

There are others for whom the influence of a great and noble building is quite sacramental. By the help of the subtle influences of such places they are lifted beyond all the things of sense and come to enjoy essential communion with God. I know at least one staunch Scottish Protestant for whom the Westminster Cathedral has a quite unique value as a help to prayer. He is more distracted than helped by ritual, but a quiet vastness such as that great building now provides is of priceless use to him.

Others, again, plainly find that ritual does help them. Alone and at home they have only faint experiences of God in prayer, but in His temples and while rich and ornate worship is offered by many persons they are lifted beyond themselves and find His face. To a great many that experience comes to its highest when they partake of the Communion.

On the other hand, for people of a different temperament buildings and ritual are quite indifferent matters. All that they need is some fellowship in prayer. Provided they can find some company of like-minded persons who will with them wait on God they are satisfied. Some of them confess that alone they remain spiritually impotent. Distracting thoughts and a sense of personal incompetence make their private devotions of little value. But common worship lifts them into God's presence, and they know Him for themselves though also in company with others. And there are still others who need nothing except quiet and solitude. A bare room, or a dugout, or a quiet corner in an empty and even ugly church is all that they need. With closed eyes and ears at rest they can get away from this world and pass into His presence who soothes and restores and guides. No special postures help them. They ask only to be allowed such bodily positions as will enable them to forget the body. And at the opposite pole from them

there are I think people to whom God is most real
when they are in crowds. They find Him through
humanity. When closely surrounded by His children they become aware of their Father in heaven.
They could tell you of places in particular streets
where they found Him and so attained to real
prayer even amid the hum and dust of the traffic.

These are at least a few of the ways in which
men learn to pray. All of them, however, are
secondary to the supreme way. "For this world
the word of God is Christ." We cannot see God,
but "we see Jesus." In Jesus for the simplest God
is made manifest. Through Jesus God becomes a
real and knowable person. And therefore beyond
all other ways Jesus is the way into a sense of
God's presence. In other words, it is by thinking
about Jesus that most people attain to a sense of
God's reality. Apart from Him God remains to us
so much of a mystery that it is hard to have any
sense of His nearness. But in Jesus men saw and
handled the word of life. By fellowship with Him
they attained to fellowship with God. And so it
is still. It may not seem so to those who have had
no experience of the matter. They may be tempted
to say they do not see how thinking about an historical person can bring a present sense of God's nearness and reality. But the answer to that is supplied
by experience. As a matter of fact, thousands find
that thought about Jesus *does* introduce them to the
Divine presence. That is what they mean when
they say in prayer that they approach God "through
Christ." When this world seems to them merely

material, hard, and irresponsive, they go back in
thought to that life in which God was made manifest, and at once their spiritual natures are quickened so that they know themselves in the presence
of their Father in heaven.

Yes, Jesus is the way to the Father; and though
we may find that other means also help us to realize
God, yet even with them it is probable that the very
content we put into the word "God" is supplied by
the historical Jesus.   When men stand alone before
the face of nature and are moved to their depths by
the sense of the Divine presence, they probably read
into nature more than is there.   Their exaltation
comes not merely from the sense of *a* presence, but
from the sense that the presence which disturbs
them is the one they know already through Jesus.

The question of words will no doubt trouble
some.   Possibly many will be helped by using set
forms of words, so long as they take care to put
sincere meaning into them.   Others may find that
they do not need words.   The Psalmists advise us
at times to be "silent towards God."   Others, again,
will find their own words without difficulty.   Once
more let each of us find out for ourselves what we
need.   The matter is worth a great deal of trouble.
If we really want to help in building the Kingdom,
we may even come to believe that it is of more
importance thus to secure food for the soul, than
to make certain of our daily meals.

I would fain add a word of caution lest any of
us disparage the means and methods of prayer
which others use, but which do not happen to help

us, or be necessary to us. Those who do not get help through church services are apt to be scornful of those who do. Those who get their help through church worship are apt to assume that all others ought to get their help in the same way. "True worshippers must worship the Father in spirit and in truth." That was Christ's final word about it. He did not care whether men worshipped at Jerusalem, or "in this mountain." One thing only is necessary and that *to find Him*. It would make greatly for religious peace in this country if we all learnt to rejoice when we hear of others finding God in any way, and ceased to insist that our way is the best. Some indeed insist that their way is the only way. We cannot be too insistent about the necessity of prayer. But we cannot be too catholic in our appreciation of the manifold forms and ways in which prayer is achieved.

The other great resource of a Christian disciple is to be found in other people. To use the common master word of our day, it is to be found in fellowship. We are so made that we need each other in all departments of life, and supremely in this one. We can and do mediate God to one another. By fellowship we rise to experiences which are impossible otherwise.

This does not merely mean fellowship with living contemporaries. The greatest spirits of all history still offer us their fellowship with royal generosity through their books. All who have lived lives of real discipleship—all who have had real experience of the Christian way—all who have conquered and many who have largely failed, still offer us help beyond all price by what they have put of themselves into their writings. Along this way, they declare, we found life: along that one we found death. By many a sorrow and many a failure, as well as by many a triumphant success, they have accumulated a store of wisdom which they share with us freely.

It is thus that the reading of the Bible comes to have such a central place in the disciple's life. He will of necessity read much and often in the gospels that he may increasingly know the mind of his Lord. But he will also read what Christ's great followers have to say about the Christian way, and he will draw from them both knowledge and inspiration. Possibly the reading of the Bible has come to seem to many a mere duty which they have been taught to perform, but which brings no real stimulus to their minds. But that is because it has been read merely as a duty, and perhaps in a rather mechanical way. Once we have learnt to feel in it the living beat of actual human lives, and to realize that these men were "up against" a world very like ours, we shall discover a new reality in it, and therefore a new interest.

But it is not only the men of the Bible who have living things to say to us about the Christian way. In addition to them there stands near to us a great host of men and women, not dead but merely out of sight, who offer us still their fellowship, and who have great experiences to share with us.

Not only Paul, and John, and Peter, but also Augustine and Francis, and Thomas à Kempis—Luther and Bunyan, and Brother Lawrence—Wesley, and Woolman, and William Penn—Lincoln, and Livingstone, and Shaftesbury, and so on through all the ranks of that great and varied company who have loved the same Lord, and helped in the building of His Kingdom. These people make the great cloud of witnesses who still with sympathy and understanding watch the runners of today. He is no wise man who rejects their company and remains ignorant of all they have to teach. And their company is always available. Living souls who help us may at times be inaccessible, but everywhere and always these great and humble souls wait upon us. Through the literature of Christendom they are all within reach. We may pick and choose for ourselves. No two of us will select the same special persons. But each of us may, if we will, hold converse with some chosen band of great forerunners who are able to cheer our despair, resolve many of our perplexities, and sustain us amid the ardours of the narrow way. And that is beyond all question one of the great resources of the disciple.

Then there remain the other living people who are going the same way—in other words, the fellowship of other disciples is almost always available. It is difficult to overestimate the help that they are able to afford. Absolute statements are perhaps very seldom true ones, and there possibly are exceptional people who travel wonderfully on the Christian way though they seek no fellowship with others.

They live apart and yet serve greatly. But they are the few and the peculiar. For the great mass of people a life of discipleship is well nigh impossible except in fellowship. It is one of the deepest of our instincts to seek the company of others when specially hard things have to be done. And discipleship always means specially hard things. Just as the other men in his platoon became for many a soldier the power that carried him through the terrors and abominations of the front, so in the Christian warfare it is the inspiration of the company of other soldiers that makes the campaign a possibility.

To begin with, we need others for the enrichment and correction of our thinking about Christian issues. No one man ever saw all sides of truth. Perhaps no company of people can see all sides of it. But they can at least see a great many more than any individual. Probably we are only now beginning to discover all the value that there is in corporate thinking. What really explains the recent multiplication of conferences of many kinds is just the fact that when a number of people in any truly intimate way set themselves to seek after truth, they help each other to a larger view of it than is possible in any other way. When men and women, of various ages and of various types, all alike contribute what they know to a sincere discussion, the result is often a very rich one. One by one we are a prey to our own prejudices. Together we may surmount them if we will. It is the peculiar snare of deeply religious persons, to which perhaps the

most earnest are most exposed, that they should
think that all religious experience ought to be of the
same type as their own, and that all people ought
to see truth as they see it. But such private obses-
sions become impossible when men and women find
themselves in the company of others whose spiritual
power is beyond all question, but whose convictions
and experiences vary widely.

Then, further, most men find in time that they
need the stimulus which comes to them from the
faith and courage of others, and are immensely
strengthened by association with those who are also
trying to attain to discipleship. It is one thing to
resolve to let all else go and follow the way of the
Kingdom, but it is quite another to maintain that
resolve amid "the coiled perplexities" of our complicated modern life, and when subjected to all the
strains for heart and head which belong to any
modern calling. There are few who are not at
times tempted to give in, and fewer still who do
not find that their courage sometimes flags. At
times it seems difficult to be even interested in the
things we had meant to care about always. A
certain paralysis of feeling is apt to descend upon
us, and all the glow seems to go out of our beliefs
and purposes. The case for cynicism will seem
very strong, and the case for an easy-going attitude
to life stronger still.

And then it is that through the fellowship of
our fellow travellers the greatest of boons may
come to us. As they allow us to share their life,
new life seems to flow into us. By the influence of

one belief is made clear again.   Another seems able
almost to bestow courage, and a third helps us to
realize the presence of God once more.   Men who
had been feeling that they could not pray, find
themselves able to pray as the opportunity comes to
them to be uplifted by the prayers of others.   Men
who had felt utterly drained of all enthusiasm find
their empty beings filled when subjected to the
contagion of the keenness of others.   And so in the
spiritual world we help each other up steep and
slippery places, and find life growing richer and
fuller as we give and take in the interchange of
common life.   I do not think that mere fellowship
with others can ever take the place of those quiet
hours of solitude in which a man must face his
God, and get back at all costs to sincerity and
reality.   I think there is an inner chamber in every
life into which no others ought to enter.   There
are reserves of the soul to maintain which belongs
to spiritual chastity.   And no doubt there is a danger
that men may try to live exclusively on fellowship
and delude themselves into supposing they believe
and feel when they are really only handling the
convictions and feelings of others at second hand.
Fellowship has its dangers as all other good things
have.   He who *only* realizes God when he is with
others who have done it first, might do well to
doubt whether he has yet found God.   Thousands
of people have probably ere this lived all their lives
upon the emotions which church produced in them
without having any sincere religion that was truly
their own.   "It is a sad reflection," says Penn, "that

many men have no religion, and that most men have none of their own." Seeing which it is not to be wondered at that Penn should counsel us to seek the fruits of solitude. It is well after having shared in the religious activities of a group to ask oneself whether one has really any truly personal faith.

And yet all that admitted, it remains true that fellowship is one of the main ways in which the grace of God is ministered and mediated to us, and no man who really means to be a disciple can afford to live spiritually alone.

And thirdly, it is surely plain that we need others if ever we are to take an effective share in the practical labours which the building of the Kingdom involves. The great tasks of reconstruction which now await us are all of them such as can only be achieved by numbers of men and women working in concert. They defy the isolated individual. In order to count a man must get into his place in the body of Christ. Just as a great building requires architects, and measurers, and labourers and skilled tradesmen of a score of different sorts and is a flat impossibility either to the individual or to a disunited mass of workers, so in the building of the Kingdom unless we work with others, and according to some concerted scheme, we can achieve nothing. That, at least, is so plain that I need not elaborate it further.

It is all these facts that justify the statement that a real Christian life cannot be an individual thing. It is essentially and necessarily a social thing. We must advance together or not at all. All the great Christian acts are social acts. We pray to *our* Father. It is *our* daily bread for which we ask. It is *our* sins that we present to God for forgiveness. It is for each other that we break the bread in the central sacrament of our faith. St. Paul has expressed this by saying that a member of the body separate from the body is a useless thing. The life of a Christian is like the life of a hand or a foot. It depends vitally on the life of the whole organism to which it belongs.

Another way of saying this is to say that Church is unalterably and eternally necessary to those who would fain be disciples. The Church came into existence because men and women who wanted to follow Christ found that they needs must hold together, and thus they made the Church by inevitable instinct. The Church came into being just because there were would-be Christians in the world. And the Church will always come into being whenever and wherever there are would-be Christians in the world. Were all the existing churches destroyed tomorrow others would spring into being at once, unless all Christians had been destroyed too, and, indeed, unless the spirit of Christ should cease to call men and women unto Him.

But when I say the Church, I mean just and only companies of would-be followers. When I say that a man must join a church to live a Christian life, I mean only that he must get into fellowship with others, few or many, of like mind with himself. I do not mean that he either should or can find the great essential help in any particular church. Here, again, all the infinite varieties of human nature must be remembered, and just as men differ widely in the matter of prayer—some requiring this kind of help and some another, so also in this matter of Church. The real Church universal presents itself to men today in a vast variety of differing forms. Some will be at home in one chamber of that vast building, and some in another. The differing forms of the Church really constitute its wealth. To force all men into churches of one uniform pattern would be like putting them into straight jackets, in which the majority of them would perish. The God who designed our rich humanity, which manifests itself in such uncounted variations of type, must also have designed that the churches which His children should form would also be almost infinite in variety.

And yet this also is true, that a clique can never be a church. An exclusive group can never be a church, any more than an exclusive spirit can be a Christian. People may draw together by irresistible affinity, but unless they maintain an attitude of great hospitality towards all others they will find that Christ is no longer dwelling with them. He will go to any place which is free to all His brethren, but He will go to no abode that shuts Him off from the common life of humanity. As we seek after a fellowship that may help us in the difficulties of personal living, we are all tempted to be both very critical and very sensitive. We do not like this church because the people seem cold, or that one because the people are demonstrative, or another because the people seem to us ignorant. But it would be well to ask ourselves at such times whether we have really ever discovered our brethren, and are really willing to belong loyally to the great family of God. They must have been a very rough, noisy, and ignorant band who first surrounded Jesus, and those who would not mingle with that band never got near Him. The wise and the mighty of this world have seldom cared truly about Him. His people have generally seemed without honour and without distinction. He loved the people so much that those who cannot love the people disagree with Him. Perhaps the great first lesson which confronts many of us is, then, just a lesson in learning to appreciate the very people with whom Christ lived and for whom He died. And when that lesson has been learnt the difficulty of finding "a church that suits us" may be found to have disappeared. He who really loves his neigh-bour will never feel uncomfortable in his neigh-bour's church. Church was never meant to soothe our æsthetic sensibilities, or to conform to our in-stincts of social exclusiveness. It is designed to offer us an opportunity of honest fellowship with other people who are going our way in the spiritual life. Unless we will march with the army we can-not march at all.

What I have been trying to say in this chapter is just that the resources of a disciple are to be found partly in God and partly in his fellow-men. They are found in God when He is realized through prayer, and they are found in our fellow-men when we achieve any fellowship with them that is honest and warm-hearted. And these two essential resources are not in the last resort two but one. The nearer we get to God the more truly are we inclined to, and fitted for, fellowship with others. And the more real our fellowship with others, the more intense will our love and loyalty to God become.

"If we walk in the light . . . we have fellowship one with another."

"If a man love not his brother whom he hath seen, he cannot love God whom he hath not seen."

God 70
Nature 71
Union with Christ 80-81.

Sin & grace × Ch. VII